"I WON'T LEARN FROM YOU"
AND OTHER THOUGHTS ON CREATIVE MALADJUSTMENT

OTHER TITLES BY HERB KOHL INCLUDE:

The Age of Complexity (1965)

The Language and Education of the Deaf (1967)

Teaching the Unteachable (1967)

36 Children (1967)

The Open Classroom (1969)

*Golden Boy as Anthony Cool:
A Photo Essay on Names and Graffiti* (1972)

*Reading: How To—A People's Guide to Alternative Ways
of Teaching and Testing Reading* (1973)

Half the House (1974)

On Teaching (1976)

View from the Oak, with Judith Kohl (1977)

Growing with Your Children (1978)

A Book of Puzzlements (1981)

Basic Skills (1982)

Pack, Band and Colony, with Judith Kohl (1983)

Whatever Became of Emmett Gold, with Erica Kohl (1983)

Growing Minds: On Becoming a Teacher (1985)

Mathematical Puzzlements (1987)

Making Theater: Developing Plays with Young People (1988)

The Question Is College (1989)

The Long Haul (1990)

*From Archetype to Zeitgeist: An Essential Guide
to Powerful Ideas* (1992)

"I Won't Learn from You"

and Other Thoughts on Creative Maladjustment

Herbert Kohl

The New Press

Requests for permission to reproduce selections from this book
should be mailed to: Permissions Department, The New Press,
120 Wall Street, 31st floor, New York, NY 10005

Published in the United States by The New Press, New York
Distributed by Two Rivers Distribution

ISBN 978-1-56584-096-6
L.C. 93083618

The New Press publishes books that promote and enrich public discussion and
understanding of the issues vital to our democracy and to a more equitable
world. These books are made possible by the enthusiasm of our readers; the
support of a committed group of donors, large and small; the collaboration
of our many partners in the independent media and the not-for-profit sector;
booksellers, who often hand-sell New Press books; librarians; and above all by
our authors.

www.thenewpress.com

Printed in the United States of America

Contents

Foreword to the 1995 Edition

I read through *I Won't Learn From You* last night, and having just put it down, I keep thinking of Herb's great-uncle Julius playing Paul Robeson for him in the back room of a delicatessen. It is one of the rich details that lend this book a warm and loving texture.

There are many wonderful things here, including a strong rebuttal of the E. D. Hirsch agenda and the madness about "political correctness." For teachers, of course, the book is invaluable—one of the most important books on teaching published in many years. For people who know Herb, however, it has another dividend. It brings out all the sweetness and the passion and the zest for life and mischief-making humor of an infinitely vulnerable and honest human being who has made it his vocation to peddle hope in the face of despair—a task more essential today, I think, than at any time in twenty years. All in all, this is a wise and tender book, written with the deepest love for children. I will go back to it again and again for strength in future years.

JONATHAN KOZOL

Foreword

I met Herb Kohl in 1966 when we shared an office at Columbia University's Teachers College. He worked in Harlem, I worked on the Lower East Side. We were both consumed by the possibility of social transformation through education and schooling—and we both recognized that the ideal we espoused, of schools working for all children in the society, meant a new opportunity and a new challenge.

In this book, Herb once again rises to that challenge. Above, all, Herb Kohl is a teacher in these essays. In each, he opens his classroom door and the corridors of his mind and heart, too. He realizes that he has to go back to his own education to learn and teach about teaching.

In "I Won't Learn from You," "The Tattooed Man," and "Creative Maladjustment," we see Herb learning about himself in his encounters with students—and learning about himself means (as it does for most of us) recognizing the "other" in one's self. Having himself grown up the target of disparaging labels, Herb now simply assumes his students' strengths, despite institutional and social definitions to the contrary. Since such a small proportion of school children are in fact organically impaired, Herb's faith in them is a safe bet.

But what he does in response is not at all safe—taking the risk of self-revelation and close connection, and embodying the promise of public education to benefit all children and the belief that it is the teacher's job to serve that agenda. Here Herb's focus on "dreaming" is key. For him optimism is a fundamental pedagogical stance: Hope is a powerful engine that can ignite flashes of its own force. This is not merely high expectations. Hope, in Herb Kohl's lexicon, is actually recognizing the potential for change and growth in—and contribution from—those with whom he works. Herb's major resource is his ability to see his students, to see through the public presentation of self. And, in instance after instance, seeing is believing—believing in their capacity to learn.

Herb is more deeply personal in these essays than ever. He recognizes that he must return to his own ethnicity in order to connect to the sources of identity in the lives he touches. And he also understands that ethnic roots are not usefully recalled if they serve as fixed poles to be grabbed fiercely and exclusively. Instead he sees that the teaching environment is fundamentally affected by ethnic experience—and not just one's own. Belief in the significance—for good or ill—of ethnic roots is a powerful factor in Herb's approach and commitment to what he calls "the struggle for public education."

Finally, Herb brings us back to two fundamental questions. One, the short-term question: How can we survive and prosper amid bureaucratized stigma, with only a flickering light of resources, social purpose, and public values at the end of the tunnel? Two, the long-term question: How can we change the existing system in the direction of its best rhetoric and its best examples of good schooling, effective teaching, and social learning?

We live in a period when many reform ideas involve moving public education into the private and for-profit sectors. The call to take funds out of government and take government out of education seems sometimes to be the only solution high and wide enough to solve public education's colossal problems. Herb's voice warns us of the foolhardiness of that and other related notions, reminding us of the consequences of letting private privilege and economics further displace public purpose. In this inspiring collection, Herb Kohl is calling us back to equity in education, to the promises made to this country's children back when Herb and I were together at Teachers College—promises that are no less powerful and pressing today.

COLIN GREER
President, The New World Foundation

Preface

Not-learning, hopemongering, and creative maladjustment are on my mind these days. Not-learning is the conscious decision not to learn something that you could learn. It consists, for example, of refusing to learn how to cheat on your taxes, cook crack cocaine, or yield to community pressure to become racist or sexist—choosing not to learn something that you find morally offensive or personally noxious. Hopemongering is the affirmation of hope and the dream of a just and equitable future despite all the contrary evidence provided by experience. Creative maladjustment is the art of not becoming what other people want you to be and learning, in difficult times, to affirm yourself while at the same time remaining caring and compassionate.

These three concepts presuppose a fundamental belief that we all have freedom of choice and free will, and that each of us is responsible for the kind of person he becomes and for the way he treats others. Not-learning, hopemongering, and creative maladjustment are the guiding principles of my teaching and my personal life—principles sometimes difficult to maintain, but nevertheless persistent and insistent in their demands on everyday life.

The essays in this book are reflections on the complexity of holding to one's dreams. *I Won't Learn from You* was written a few years ago, but I have been thinking about some of the stories and ideas in it for over twenty years. The ideas in it are rooted in my childhood and my teaching. There have been times when I've been unable to speak about what I've experienced, when events have overwhelmed my ability to understand or communicate them. The story of Akmir, which I've tried to tell in the title essay, has troubled me for years, and I probably would not have written it if other youngsters I know these days had not been living through the same pain Akmir experienced in his short life.

"The Tattooed Man" was equally difficult for me to write because it had to do with why I became a public school teacher and why I continue to teach and care about public schools after seeing so many public schools that don't work. Writing it took me back to my childhood dreams and fantasies, and to my own experiences as a student in the New York City public schools. The essay is not just about schools. It is as much about how one comes back home to serve the community after having left, how childhood shapes vocation, and how moral values become everyday principles. It is the most personal writing I have ever done.

The essays on equity and political correctness are part of my ongoing attempt to clarify the way we talk about children and learning and oppose stigmatization of all kinds. They are attempts to engage people in the continuing struggle for social and economic justice, and to place it in the context of teaching and learning.

The final essay, "Creative Maladjustment," is about the need to remain within public education while trying to transform it. It is an attempt to show, through stories, the ways in which positive changes can be made within systems that seem unmoveable and dysfunctional.

All of these essays are extended stories, teaching and learning tales. They provide approximations to theories and expositions of ideas based on my experiences and those of people I've been privileged to work with or work for. Taken together they proclaim the abiding importance of teaching hope, resisting arbitrary authority, and taking control of one's own learning. They are my way of sharing the problems and rewards of trying to do decent work in a too-often indecent society and of affirming the importance of all our stories.

Acknowledgments

Working with The New Press has been a thorough pleasure for me. I want to thank André Schiffrin for his constant support and inspiration, and Diane Wachtell, my editor, for the intelligent, patient, sensitive, and fine work she has put into this book. I also want to thank Max Gordon, Akiko Takano, and all of the other people at The New Press who have helped me. It's a delight to be part of a publishing house that loves books and cares about ideas.

Thanks to Mike Rose, Colin Greer, Lisa Delpit, and John Caddy, who have read and criticized early versions of these essays and whose input and criticism have been kind, helpful, and influential in shaping their final form. In addition I want to thank my agent, Wendy Weil, for her support and for her insights about my work.

I would also like to thank Emily Buchwald and Milkweed Editions for publishing a chapbook version of *I Won't Learn from You*; Jack Zipes and *The Lion and the Unicorn* (Johns Hopkins University Press) for publishing an earlier version of my essay on political correctness; and Frank Pignatelli and the Second Annual

Yearbook of the Bank Street College of Education (Corwin Press) for publishing a version of the essay on equity and equality.

Finally, I want to thank my family—Tonia, Erica, Josh, Haruko, and my wife, Judy—for their loving support during all of the ups and downs of writing these essays and for the abiding intelligence and sensitivity they always bring to reading and critiquing my writing.

I Won't Learn from You

YEARS AGO, ONE of my fifth-grade students told me that his grandfather Wilfredo wouldn't learn to speak English. He said that no matter how hard you tried to teach him, Wilfredo ignored whatever words you tried to teach and forced you to speak to him in Spanish. When I got to know his grandfather, I asked, in Spanish, whether I could teach him English, and he told me unambiguously that he did not want to learn. He was frightened, he said, that his grandchildren would never learn Spanish if he gave in like the rest of the adults and spoke English with the children. Then, he said, they would not know who they were. At the end of our conversation he repeated adamantly that nothing could make him learn to speak English, that families and cultures could not survive if the children lost their parents' language and finally that learning what others wanted you to learn can sometimes destroy you.

When I discussed Wilfredo's reflections with several friends, they interpreted his remarks as a cover-up of either his fear of trying to learn English or his failure to do so. These explanations, however, show a lack of respect for Wilfredo's ability to judge what is appropriate learning for himself and for his grandchildren. By attributing failure to Wilfredo and by refusing to acknowledge the loss his family would experience through not knowing Spanish, they turned a cultural problem into a personal psychological problem: they turned willed refusal to learn into failure to learn.

I've thought a lot about Wilfredo's conscious refusal to learn English and have great sympathy for his decision. I grew up in a partially bilingual family, in a house shared by my parents, born in New York City, and my grandparents, born in the Yiddish-speaking Polish part of the Pale of Jewish Settlement in Eastern Europe. I know what it is like to face the problem of not-learning and the dissolution of culture. In addition, I have encountered willed not-learning throughout my thirty years of teaching and believe that such not-learning is often and disastrously mistaken for failure to learn or the inability to learn.

Learning how to not-learn is an intellectual and social challenge; sometimes you have to work very hard at it. It consists of an active, often ingenious, willful rejection of even the most compassionate and well-designed teaching. It subverts attempts at remediation as much as it rejects learning in the first place. It was through insight into my own not-learning that I began to understand the inner world of students who chose to not-learn what I wanted to teach. Over the years I've come to side with them in their refusal to be molded by a hostile society and have come to look upon not-learning as positive and healthy in many situations.

Before looking in detail at some of my students' not-learning and the intricate ways in which it was part of their self-respect and identity, I want to share one of my own early ventures into not-learning and self-definition. I cannot speak Yiddish, though I have had opportunities to learn from the time I was born. My father's parents spoke Yiddish most of the time, and since my family lived downstairs from them in a two-family house for fourteen of my first seventeen years, my failure to learn wasn't from lack of exposure. My father speaks both Yiddish and English and never indicated that he wouldn't teach me Yiddish. Nor did he ever try to coerce me to learn the language, so I never had educational traumas associated with learning Yiddish. My mother and her family had everything to do with it. They didn't speak Yiddish at all. Learning Yiddish meant being party to conversations that excluded my mother. I didn't reject my grandparents and their language. It's just that I didn't want to be included in conversations unless my mother was also included. In solidarity with her I learned how to not-learn Yiddish.

There was Yiddish to be heard everywhere in my environment, except at public school: on the streets, at home, in every store. Learning to not-learn Yiddish meant that I had to forget Yiddish words as soon as I heard them. When words stuck in my head, I had to refuse to associate the sounds with any meaning. If someone told a story in Yiddish, I had to talk to myself quietly in English or hum to myself. If a relative greeted me in Yiddish, I responded with the uncomprehending look I had rehearsed for those occasions. I also remember learning to concentrate on the component sounds of words and thus shut out the speaker's meaning or intent. In doing so I allowed myself to be satisfied with understanding the emotional flow of a conversation without knowing what people were saying. I was doing just the reverse of what beginning readers are expected to do—read words and understand meanings instead of getting stuck on particular letters and the sounds they make. In effect, I used phonics to obliterate meaning.

In not-learning Yiddish, I had to ignore phrases and gestures, even whole conversations, as well as words. And there were many lively, interesting conversations upstairs at my grandparents'. They had meetings about union activities, talked about family matters and events in Europe and later in Israel. They discussed articles in the *Daily Forward*, the Yiddish newspaper, and plays downtown in the Yiddish theater. Everyone was a poet, and everybody had an opinion. I let myself read hands and faces, and I imagined ideas and opinions bouncing around the room. I experienced these conversations much in the way I learned to experience Italian opera when I was fourteen. I had a sense of plot and character and could follow the flow and drama of personal interaction, yet I had no idea of the specifics of what was being said. To use another image: it was as if I were at a foreign-language movie with my father, my uncles, and my grandmother providing English subtitles whenever I asked for help understanding what was going on. I allowed myself to be content with this partial knowledge, but now I mourn the loss of the language and culture of my father's family that it entailed.

Deciding to actively not-learn something involves closing off part of oneself and limiting one's experience. It can require actively refusing to pay attention, acting dumb, scrambling one's thoughts, and overriding curiosity. The balance of gains and losses resulting from such a turning away from experience is difficult to assess. I still can't tell how much I gained or lost by not-learning Yiddish. I know that I lost a language that would have enriched my life, but I gained an understanding of the psychology of active not-learning that has been very useful to me as a teacher.

Because not-learning involves willing rejection of some aspect of experience, it can often lead to what appears to be failure. For example, in the case of some youngsters, not-learning to read can be confused with failing to learn to read if the rejection of learning is overlooked as a significant factor. I had that happen to me when I was eleven and expanded not-learning Yiddish to not-learning Hebrew. I was sent to *chedar*, Hebrew school, to learn that part of the Torah that I would have to read aloud in front of the whole congregation during my bar mitzvah. My family was not at all religious, and though we belonged to a temple, we attended services only on Yom Kippur. From my perspective the point of

4

going to Hebrew school was not to learn Hebrew but to ensure that I didn't embarrass my parents when I had to recite part of the Torah at my bar mitzvah. As I figured it, if I not-learned Hebrew, it would save me a lot of effort and time I could use for science projects and my rather tentative experiments with writing. And so for two years I applied what I had learned about not-learning Yiddish and I not-learned Hebrew. I could read the sounds and recite my way through the *Mahzor*, the daily prayer book, and the Torah. I listened to our teacher-rabbi drone on about the righteousness of the Jews and our special role in history, and I was silent though cynical.

I did, however, get in trouble for my arrogant not-learning. One day the rabbi gave us a test with questions written in Hebrew. Since I couldn't translate a word from Hebrew to English, much less an entire question, my prospects for passing the test were not good. I was too proud to show the rabbi that I couldn't do the test, so I set it up with my friend Ronnie that I would copy his test. Cheating in Hebrew school was not a moral issue to me but a matter of saving face. Ronnie understood my dilemma perfectly and told me he would have loved to not-learn Hebrew too, only his father insisted on testing him every night on his Hebrew school lessons.

During the test I succeeded in copying Ronnie's whole paper, which I knew was a sure A, only I failed worse than if I had written letters at random in mock Hebrew on the test sheet. The rabbi returned all of the papers except Ronnie's and mine. Then he called the class to attention and said he felt a need to give special appreciation to Ronnie, for not only had Ronnie gotten one A, he also received a second A which, the rabbi said, was the first time in his career that any student had done that well. And, he added, Herbert didn't hand in any paper at all, which he told the class was worse than trying and failing. It seems that I had copied Ronnie's paper so accurately that I had answered the Hebrew question "What is your name?" with Ronnie's Hebrew name. I was thoroughly humiliated in front of all of my friends and, for all my arrogance about getting away with not-learning Hebrew, felt very stupid.

I never forgot this humiliation, and when I became a teacher, I resolved never to humiliate any of my students. I also decided to assume that there were complex factors behind any apparent failure which, if understood, could be used to transform it into positive learning. Not-learning Yiddish and Hebrew has made me very sensitive to the difference between not-learning and failing to learn. Failure is characterized by the frustrated will to know, whereas not-learning involves the will to refuse knowledge. Failure results from a mismatch between what the learner wants to do and is able to do. The reasons for failure may be personal, social, or cultural, but whatever they are, the results of failure are most often a loss of self-confidence accompanied by a sense of inferiority and inadequacy. Not-learning produces thoroughly different effects. It tends to strengthen the will, clarify one's definition of self, reinforce self-discipline, and provide inner satisfaction. Not-learning can also get one in trouble if it results in defiance or a refusal to become socialized in ways that are sanctioned by the dominant authority.

Not-learning tends to take place when someone has to deal with unavoidable challenges to her or his personal and family loyalties, integrity, and identity. In such situations there are forced choices and no apparent middle ground. To agree to learn from a stranger who does not respect your integrity causes a major loss of self. The only alternative is to not-learn and reject the stranger's world.

In the course of my teaching career I have seen children choose to not-learn many different skills, ideas, attitudes, opinions, and values. At first I confused not-learning with failing. When I had youngsters in my classes who were substantially "behind" in reading, I assumed that they had failed to learn how to read. Therefore, I looked for the sources of their failure in the reading programs they were exposed to, in their relationships with teachers and other adults in authority, and in the social and economic conditions of their lives. I assumed that something went wrong when they faced a written text, that either they made errors they didn't know how to correct or they were the victims of bad teaching.

Other causes of failure I searched for were mismatches between the students' language and the language of the schools or between the students' experiences and the kind of experience presupposed by their teachers or the reading texts. In all of these cases I assumed that my students had failed at something they had tried to do. Sometimes I was correct, and then it was easy to figure out a strategy to help them avoid old errors and learn, free of failure. But there were many cases I came upon where obviously intelligent students were beyond success or failure when it came to reading or other school-related learning. They had consciously placed themselves outside the entire system that was trying to coerce or seduce them into learning and spent all their time and energy in the classroom devising ways of not-learning, short-circuiting the business of failure altogether. They were engaged in a struggle of wills with authority, and what seemed to be at stake for them was nothing less than their pride and integrity. Most of them did not believe that they were failures or that they were inferior to students who succeeded on the schools' terms, and they were easy to distinguish from the wounded self-effacing students who wanted to learn but had not been able to do so.

I remember one student, Barry, who was in one of my combined kindergarten and first-grade classes in Berkeley in the 1970s. He had been held back in the first grade by his previous teacher for being uncooperative, defiant, and "not ready for the demands of second grade." He was sent to my class because it was multi-age-graded, and the principal hoped I could get him to catch up and go on with other students his age by the end of the year. Barry was confident and cocky but not rude. From his comments in class it was clear that he was quite sensitive and intelligent. The other students in the class respected him as the best fighter and athlete in class, and as a skilled and funny storyteller.

During the first week of school, one of the students mentioned to me that their teacher the previous year had been afraid of Barry. I've seen a number of cases where white teachers treat very young African-American boys as if they were seventeen, over six feet tall, addicted to drugs, and menacing. Barry was a victim of that manifestation of racism. He had evidently been given the run of the school the previous year—had been allowed to wander the halls at will, refuse participation in group activities, and avoid any semblance of academic work. Consequently, he fell behind and was not promoted from first to second grade.

The first time I asked Barry to sit down and read with me, he threw a temper tantrum and called me all kinds of names. We never got near a book. I had to relate to his behavior, not his reading. There was no way for me to discover the level of his skills or his knowledge of how reading works. I tried to get him to read a few more times and watched his responses to me very carefully. His tantrums clearly were manufactured on the spot. They were a strategy of not-reading. He never got close enough to a book to have failed to learn how to read.

The year before, this response had the effect he wanted. He was let alone and, as a bonus, gained status in the eyes of the other children as being someone teachers feared. Not-reading, as tragic as it might become in his future, was very successful for him as a kindergartner. My job as a teacher was to get him to feel more empowered by reading than by practicing his active not-learning to read.

I developed a strategy of empowerment for Barry and didn't

even bother to think about remediation. I was convinced he could learn to read perfectly well if he assented to learn how to read. The strategy was simple and involved a calculated risk. I decided to force him to read with me and then make it appear to other members of the class that he could read well, and that his past resistance was just a game he controlled. The goal was to have him show me up in class, as if his past failure was a joke he was playing on us all, and have him display to the entire class a reading ability he didn't know he had.

I prepared myself for a bit of drama. One Monday afternoon I asked Barry to come read with me. Naturally, all the other students stopped what they were doing and waited for the show. They wanted to see if Barry would be able to not-read one more time. He looked at me, then turned around and walked away. I picked up a book, went over to him, gently but firmly sat him down in a chair, and sat down myself. Before he could throw the inevitable tantrum, I opened the book and said, "Here's the page you have to read. It says, 'This is a bug. This is a jug. This is a bug in the jug.' Now read it to me." He started to squirm and put his hands over his eyes. Only I could see a sly grin forming as he sneaked a look at the book. I had given him the answers, told him exactly what he had to do to show me and the rest of the class that he knew how to read all along. It was his decision: to go on playing his not-learning game or accept my face-saving gift and open up the possibility of learning to read. I offered him the possibility of entering into a teaching-learning relationship with me without forcing him to give up any of his status, and fortunately he accepted the gift. He mumbled, "This is a bug, this is a jug, this is a bug in a jug," then tossed the book on the floor and, turning to one of the other children, said defiantly, "See, I told you I already know how to read."

This ritual battle was repeated all week and into the next, subsiding slowly as he felt that the game was no longer necessary and that he was figuring out the relationship of letters to sounds, words, and meanings. After a while, reading became just another one of the things that Barry did in class. I never did any remedial teaching or treated him as a failed reader. In fact, I was able to reach him by acknowledging his choice to not-learn and by tricking him out of it. However, if he had refused assent, there is no way I could have forced him to learn to read. That was a very important lesson to me. It helped me understand the essential role that will and free choice play in learning, and it taught me the importance of considering people's stance toward learning in the larger context of the choices they make as they create lives and identities for themselves.

Over the years, I've known many youngsters who chose to actively not-learn what their school, society, or family tried to teach them. Not all of them were potential victims of their own choices to not-learn. For some, not-learning was a strategy that made it possible for them to function on the margins of society instead of falling into madness or total despair. It helped them build a small, safe world in which their feelings of being rejected by family and society could be softened. Not-learning played a positive role and enabled them to take control of their lives and get through difficult times. Recently, I encountered a young man I've known since he was in elementary school who has become a master of not-learning and has turned it into an artistic life form. Rick, who is nineteen, has consciously chosen to reject the conventional values of middle-class life. Through his poetry, he scorns and criticizes such pious values as hard work, obedience, patriotism, loyalty, and money. He honed his not-learning skills in elementary school and became particularly adept at them in junior high school. An articulate, conscious not-learner, Rick is very explicit about his achievements. He claims that the most difficult not-learning he ever did was in introductory algebra, which he failed three times. Rick is very quick in math, and there were no intellectual reasons he couldn't learn algebra.

There were emotional reasons Rick refused to learn algebra, but it's essential to distinguish here between his decision to not-learn algebra and his ability to learn it. Rick could have learned algebra quite easily. There was nothing wrong with his mind, his ability to concentrate, or his ability to deal with abstract ideas. He could read, and he did read books he chose. He knew how to do very complex building projects and science experiments. He enjoyed playing around with athletic statistics and gambling odds. He just rejected the whole idea of being tested and measured against other students and, though he was forced to attend school, there was no way to force him to perform. He refused to learn and through that refusal gained power over his parents and teachers. As a free autonomous individual, he chose to not-learn, and that was what his parents and the school authorities didn't know how to deal with.

It's interesting how stuck parents and school authorities are on a single way to live and learn. Any youngster who refuses to perform as demanded is treated as a major threat to the entire system. Experts are consulted, complex personal or family causes are fabricated, special programs are invented, all to protect the system from changing itself and accommodating difference. People like Rick then get channeled into marginal school experiences and, too often, marginalized lives.

Rick told me that not-learning algebra was an intriguing challenge, since he felt that the abstract representation of complex mathematical relationships might interest him as much as chess did. In order to force failure Rick found ingenious ways to dissolve equations into marks on the page by creating visual exercises that treated the equations as nonmathematical markings. For example, one exercise consisted of reading an equation from the equal sign out in a number of steps so that he would read

$3a + 2b = 12a - 32$ as the sequence: $=$, $b = 1$, $2b = 12$, $+2b = 12a$, $a + 2b = 12a -$, etc. Sometimes he would even memorize the sequence.

When his teacher asked him what he was doing, he explained exactly what his procedure was, infuriating the teacher more than if he had merely said he didn't understand the problem.

Rick's rejection of authority is sincere, well thought out, and based on a personal analysis of some unsettling experiences he has had in his family life. There is fear of the world and personal insecurity in his rejection too. He believes that people should not judge each other, that they should live with minimal possessions and take pleasure from each other's company and from their own creative abilities. Rick, who is a musician, is an anarchist who lives his beliefs. He left school, moved out of his home, and now lives communally with other members of his band and a few other friends. Their ambition, in addition to making music and art, is to live free of institutional control and to restore some peace and sanity to an earth they see pulled apart by greed and competition.

Consistent with this philosophy, Rick told me that he has not-learned many things which go against his beliefs. Some of them appear extreme, but none of them harm anybody or hurt the earth though they do offend social customs. For example, he has not-learned to wear shoes and has developed a whole series of strategies so that he can manage to get into places where shoes are required or expected, such as restaurants or theaters. Rick distinguishes not-learning to wear shoes from simply refusing to wear shoes. The difference is manifested in Rick's total lack of hostility when people tell him that shoes are required or expected. Rick's response is that he's sorry about it but he can't wear shoes. In successfully not-learning to wear shoes despite the pressure on him to wear them, it's no longer an issue for him and therefore he has avoided the defiant attitude of someone who merely refuses to wear shoes.

More generally, Rick is not asking to be accepted or rejected for what he does. Being left alone to be as he pleases is enough. He has chosen how he will and won't be socialized, what he'll learn and what he'll not-learn. Many of his arguments against consumerism and the arrogant wastefulness of our society are convincing. In some ways his life is healthier and saner than the norm. Unfortunately, there are people who represent the institutions of conformity of our society and resent Rick's choice to not conform. They try to categorize, stigmatize, and even institutionalize and punish him. He refuses to learn to act according to their definitions of him. He says he'll not-learn to be crazy or criminal and won't be driven to give up his autonomy and sanity by accepting their right to invalidate his experiences and stigmatize him. I don't know how Rick will make out in the future. I worry that the rejection he has experienced will finally wear him down and that he'll turn nasty or go crazy.

It may be that he'll also find that one day he'll wish he knew things he'd not-learned. That happened to me when, in September of 1954, I left the Bronx for Harvard, encountered my first Protestants, and found myself wishing I could speak Hebrew. In my neighborhood in the Bronx and at the Bronx High School of Science, I never considered myself a member of an ethnic or racial minority, since I wasn't. Most of the people in my neighborhood and at school were Jewish. I wasn't naive—I knew that Jews were persecuted, that we were a sometimes rejected and despised ethnic minority in the United States. But on an everyday level I lived with Jews, went to school with Jews, and for the most part socialized with Jews. In my neighborhood, in addition to Jews there were Italians and Irish, and a smattering of African Americans and Puerto Ricans. In high school, my few non-Jewish friends were African-American, Irish, or Italian. Before I went to Harvard I was accustomed to living in a daily world in which I was part of the majority, and I acted and lived without that caution, suspicion, and self-consciousness minorities often develop when they have daily contact with a dominant majority.

At Harvard I soon realized that the social world was thoroughly different from the one I grew up in. Not only did white Protestant males dominate my freshman dorm (Harvard was all-male then), but I felt they enjoyed indulging that dominance by bringing up the issue of my Jewishness and of my working-class background. This may have been done in a spirit of goodwill, but I couldn't experience it that way. During all-night bull sessions I was asked about the Bronx, about Judaism, about the way my family lived, all in a way that seemed to preclude my asking them about their backgrounds. I was the curiosity, they were the norm. One student on my floor urged me to come with him to Memorial Chapel to hear Reinhold Niebuhr preach so that I could be exposed to the sophistication and relevance of contemporary Protestant thinking. Another urged me to read the New Testament, informing me that no educated person could live without knowing it. And then I remember conversations about people and places I had never heard of, prep school talk that made me feel very much a foreigner.

My problem was compounded by a number of other Jewish students who were also discovering their everyday minority status and were responding to it by becoming aggressively Jewish. They pressured me to join Hillel, the Jewish student organization, in order to alleviate some of the stress by spending time in a self-segregated Jewish environment where the illusion of being part of a majority could be reestablished.

I wanted to be myself, neither minority nor majority, and rejected both the pressure to assimilate and to separate. It was very hard to walk that thin line alone, yet there was no one to talk to about my desire to learn everything Harvard had to offer without giving up myself. And I thought a lot about my father's parents those days. They had come from Eastern Europe through

Germany and England to the United States. They didn't try to assimilate and didn't fall into any protective religious orthodoxy. My grandfather maintained his socialist vision of one big union of all peoples and cultures and must have thought about the problems I was now facing. If only I could speak to him intimately, personally, find out his ideas, learn his thoughts about his own experiences and hear his words, not as songs or through translations, but as meanings. I wished I spoke Yiddish and felt angry at myself for having willfully refused to learn it. Only when it was too late did I understand what I had lost by not-learning Yiddish. The voice I needed to hear and to call on in my own musings about identity was not there for me. I managed to limp along and after a while discovered, first through reading, and later through traveling and finding friends, voices and people that helped me understand how to cross boundaries of class and culture without losing my own identity. However, I'm convinced that it has been a longer and more painful voyage than it might have been had I known the language my grandparents spoke.

Akmir, a young African-American man I had the privilege of knowing for the last three years of his life, was wiser than I was and struggled to learn and maintain his culture and learn his roots despite a racist school system that he was required to attend. In school he was a passionate not-learner. I remember his telling me of spending a semester in a junior high school social studies class not merely not-learning the subject but actively trying to destroy the teacher's and the textbook's credibility. Akmir had joined a militant separatist group that was an offshoot of the Nation of Islam. They believed that they were among the 7 percent of African Americans who understood the truth that the white man was a devil and had to be ruthlessly rooted out and destroyed. One of their goals was purifying Harlem of all whites.

Akmir's experiences with whites did very little to refute the 7 percenters' analysis. That opinion accurately applied to one of

Akmir's high school history teachers, who believed that his students—African-American and Puerto Rican—were stupid, lazy, and incapable of understanding complex ideas. He talked to the class in a condescending manner, addressing them as "you" as in "You people don't know how to hold a job," and "You people have never learned to adopt American values and that's why you can't compete in the marketplace."

Most of the students were content to not-learn what he taught by playing dumb. A few actually learned what he taught and believed that they were stupid and incapable of productive lives. Akmir and one friend, Thomas X, were actively defiant. They not only refused to learn what he taught but tried to take over the class and change the curriculum into an attack on white racism. Whenever he talked about American values, for example, they would point out that slavery was an American value according to the Constitution and would try to demonstrate that racism, not lack of intelligence or ability, was the root of black failure and poverty. The teacher tried to shut them up, referred them to the guidance counselor, sent them to the principal, and in every way but answering their challenges, tried to silence them. Nothing worked, because Akmir and Thomas X refused to accept the validity of school authority and preached to the principal and the counselors the same line they preached in class. After one semester of bitter struggle at this school, both Akmir and Thomas X were transferred to a special school for discipline problems. These were schools for youngsters who had mastered strategies of not-learning and infuriated school authorities but had done nothing wrong. The schools were created to separate, within an already racially segregated system, teachers who were failing their students from their angry victims.

I didn't know Akmir until three years after he left high school. He had passed all of his classes, but his diploma had been withheld from him for "citizenship" reasons. The principal and guidance counselor decided that he wasn't a loyal American since he raised questions that they interpreted as anti-American. They decided that he didn't deserve to graduate because of this attitude and decreed that he had to take and pass a course in citizenship sometime during the two years after his class graduated in order to receive the diploma he had rightfully earned by passing all the required courses. They also told him that sometime in the future they would decide what work or school experience could count as a citizenship class. Akmir told them what he thought of them before leaving the school for what he believed was the last time.

At the time (it was 1965), I was a graduate student at Teachers College, Columbia University, and Betty Rawls, another graduate student, and I were teaching a class in psychology for a group of high-school-aged students who were older brothers and sisters of former students of mine from Harlem. Brenda Jackson, one of the students, brought Akmir to class one day. They were a bit late, and when they arrived, the class was discussing whether Freudian ideas applied to teenagers growing up in Harlem. The discussion was quite lively, but when Brenda and Akmir came into the room, everyone fell silent. Brenda sat down, but Akmir remained standing and looked straight at me. I noticed how strong he looked, both physically and mentally.

Since everyone else in the room remained silent, I talked about my understanding of Freud and brought up some questions I had about some main Freudian concepts. After about five minutes Akmir took a few steps toward the front of the room and said quietly but fiercely, "That's white man's psychology."

I didn't disagree and suggested he go into his reasons for making that statement. He said there was no point in doing it for a white man, whereupon I told him he was wrong, adding that though Freud was a white man, he was also a bourgeois Viennese Jew who had grown up in the late 1800s and that it was unclear whether his ideas were adequate to account for the psychology of non-Jews, of working-class people, of women, and of young people in the 1960s, as well as of blacks.

He pushed aside my comments and began a harangue on racism, injustice, and the Wilderness of North America, which was the way Black Muslims referred to the United States. I grew angry and told him that the class was voluntary, that he could leave if he wanted to, but that we were there to learn together, and I wasn't bullshitting about wanting to know his ideas. Any intelligent position could be presented, defended, and argued, but learning couldn't take place without respect for everybody's voice.

The students glanced anxiously back and forth from Akmir to me. I rested my case and he smiled and said, "Well, maybe we should start with ego psychology and see what ego means for white people and for black people." I agreed, and we entered into that discussion.

After class Akmir came up and introduced himself. I told him that his questions and challenges were just what the class needed and invited him to join us. Betty and I usually assigned material to be read for each class, but since most of the students didn't get around to reading it, we began each class summarizing the issues we intended to discuss. Akmir read everything, studied it thoroughly, and came to class prepared to argue. He read all of the material aggressively, looking for sentences or phrases that indicated or could be interpreted to imply racism, ranging from uses of the words "black" or "dark" to signify evil to sophisticated arguments that implied the superiority of Western culture. For a few sessions the class was dominated by his questioning of our texts. At first I thought it was a game meant to provoke me, but it soon became clear that that was an egotistic response on my part. Akmir was hunting down American English for insinuations of racism and was trying to purify the language. He had learned some of these techniques from the Black Muslims and 7 percenters, who were very skillful in hunting out claims of European pureness and African primitivity and who understood that when sophisticated Westerners were contrasted with unsophisticated peoples of color, racism was afoot. I learned from Akmir's analyses how I too fell into sloppy, racist linguistic habits and came to take his criticisms seriously. I tried to read texts from his point of view and pick out the phrases and thoughts that he might find offensive. In some cases, it made reading familiar material very uncomfortable. I had thought of having the class analyze Conrad's *Heart of Darkness* from a psychoanalytic point of view but decided to abandon that exercise because, on rereading it with Akmir's sensitivities in mind, the explicit and offensive racism at the heart of the story appalled me. I had known before that the story could be interpreted as racist, but had always felt that that was just a secondary, unfortunate aspect of an extraordinary piece of writing. This time, though the quality of the writing wasn't diminished by my new reading, the story became repugnant to me. The racism became the primary characteristic of the writing, not a secondary one that could be understood and explained away in light of Conrad's cultural background and historical situation. And I understood that I shouldn't teach *The Heart of Darkness* unless I was ready to deal explicitly with the text's racism and condemn Conrad.

Last year, more than twenty years after this incident, I read an essay by the Nigerian novelist Chinua Achebe entitled "An Image of Africa: Racism in Conrad's *Heart of Darkness*"* that confirmed my analysis of the Conrad story. Achebe, after making his case against Conrad, states quite unambiguously, "The point of my observations should be quite clear by now, namely that Joseph Conrad was a thoroughgoing racist. That this simple truth is glossed over in criticisms of his work is due to the fact that white racism against Africa is such a normal way of thinking that its manifestations go completely unremarked."†

I learned from Akmir's reading techniques how to unlearn

---

* In Chinua Achebe, *Hopes and Impediments* (Garden City, N.Y.: Doubleday, 1989), pp. 1–20.

† Ibid., p. 11.

habits of mine that let such racism in books pass unexamined. Before knowing him, I was not attuned to many of the nuances of racist implication because I was not the victim of racism. I did not suffer through every offensive phrase I encountered when reading, nor did I experience rage when racism was cloaked in the authority of tradition or the language of excellence. The lack of that sensitivity bothered me, and I had to unlearn this insensitivity to biased yet traditional ways of speaking and writing. In addition, I had to learn how to choose my own language and learn to make the avoidance of racist reference habit. I had to think very carefully about talking about "dark intents" and "black deeds"; to avoid using comparisons like "civilized/primitive," and "sophisticated/unsophisticated"; and to eliminate characterizations like "disadvantaged" and "deprived." I had to learn to think from the perspective of someone who had not-learned racist language, and that experience has been an important part of my growth and development. Akmir's insistence upon the details of racist reference influenced how I read, speak, and write in much the same way that current feminist writing is influencing me. For me it was a matter of unlearning what could be called habits of inclusion and exclusion. Akmir's not-learning to speak or think in the racist ways of his teachers was, for him, a healthy response to racism. Unlearning racist and sexist language represents for me a similar commitment to struggle against racism and sexism in an everyday and thorough manner. It is not merely an intellectual exercise.

A few years ago in a college seminar I taught, one of the young women in the class took a stance toward not-learning sexist language that reminded me of Akmir's stance toward the language of racism. For example, she constantly corrected anyone in class who used masculine references to represent all people. She rephrased, out loud, statements such as "Man needs to do meaningful work" or "No matter what a doctor is doing, he's always on call," and she would insist upon class time to rephrase every sentence in a story or article we read to make gender references exact. I agreed with her position but was initially annoyed at the time it was taking up in class. However, when some of the male students started baiting her for being so insistent on changing their habits of thought and ridiculing her as a "liberated girl," I supported her in her struggle and resolved to let the issue take over the class, if it came to that. I decided that, for those students, it was more important to deal with gender issues than with the other educational issues we were supposed to be covering. I made gender and the power of language to mold thought the focus of the rest of the seminar. Unlearning the language of sexism with the guidance of someone who had not-learned it was a wonderful educational adventure for me and, I hope, for the rest of the students.

As a white male, I am included in the male referent of most general phrases. I feel included in, though not necessarily described by, statements such as:

Man's actions are determined by egocentric motives.

Man is a rational animal.

All men are created equal.

It is man's fate to die.

Up to about ten or fifteen years ago it never occurred to me that women might not feel included in these statements. When this lack of inclusion was first pointed out to me, I put it down to historical circumstances of no current significance—nothing to take too seriously. The use of the male pronoun "he" in sentences such as "If a person wants something, he should fight for it" seemed comfortable and ordinary. I had developed a habit of inclusion that was comfortable to me because I was included. It wasn't comfortable to the excluded, to my wife or daughters, as my student pointed out to me. She was right. Exclusion, whether based on gender, race, class, or any other category, is a way of insulting and injuring people. I taught myself to unlearn the habits of what could be called male-talk by thinking of her as a reader when I read, until sensitivity to gender reference became habit.

Unlearning racist and sexist language habits is part of the struggle against racism and sexism. I have learned new habits of inclusion and exclusion in reference. I think about nouns and pronouns and their references with greater precision than before, and I raise political questions about language in ways that have increased my insight into miseducation through language. For example, when I read "American teenagers think that," or "teachers believe that," or "the average American is," I have to stop and search for the specifics of the reference. Does the average American teenager live in Harlem or Hanover? Does the teacher work in a private school or a public school, in a rural, urban, or suburban school? Who has been honored to be the average American of the week? Claims like these, so common in the media and in school textbooks, dismiss complex issues with glib generalizations. Sloppy habits of reference lead not only to loose thinking but to the continued avoidance of dealing with social, racial, and gender issues that must be solved in order for this society to approximate its claims to democracy.

I had to unlearn to use the pronoun "he" to refer to all people. I can, however, imagine actively not-learning it just as Akmir not-learned racist language. Not-learning it would have consisted of being aware of the problem from the start, knowing as a child that adult habits of speech were biased and choosing to oppose these habits. I might have, for example, insisted on pointing out to my teacher that the title of our history book, *Man and His World*, was not merely imprecise but insulting. I could have then gone on to underline all of the incorrect references to the male and made a point of correcting the historical record. If I took the matter a step further and insisted that the issues I raised be central to our discussion of history and called for a vote to change the name of the subject to herstory-and-history, or to theirstory, it's likely that the teacher would try to shut me up, the counselor would call me a learning and discipline problem, and the principal would threaten to expel, transfer, or refer me, all of which happened to Akmir because of his project of not-learning racism.

Not-learning and unlearning are both central techniques that support changes of consciousness and help people develop positive ways of thinking and speaking in opposition to dominant forms of oppression. Not-learning in particular requires a strong will and an ability to take the kinds of pressure exerted by people whose power you choose to question. Akmir and I often talked about the quality of his school experiences. He refused to drop out. He decided that he would sit right in the Wilderness of North America and openly not-learn what was offered to him rather than simply drop out and join a total community of other nonlearners. That meant having a response to every mention and reference to race, reading and monitoring one's reading for even the slightest implications of racism, speaking very carefully and precisely, revising everything said in order to eliminate the white version of reality.

I once asked Akmir if he ever thought beyond his not-learning and the time it took up. He said that he did, that he wanted to use that not-learning to clear a space for himself to learn without feeling oppressed by words. He also wanted to write, to tell stories in a language that was positive and unselfconscious, that spoke of the life of black people without the need to qualify life by reference to white oppression. He said he wanted to write in a separated, separatist language, a postrevolutionary language. His dream was one of writing beyond race while affirming the quality of his experience and the history of his people.

His resistance to racism was the result of his vision of a world beyond racism, which he was afraid he would never see. It was this dream that propelled his not-learning. It was probably my respect for that dream and my appreciation for what I learned through the creative efforts of his not-learning that made it possible for us to become as close as we did. It was 1967, and we talked about the meaning of the Vietnam War, which he decided to resist. We also talked about how he could approach college through his strengths rather than through resistance. He wanted to learn, to become a writer and social activist, and he needed teachers who would teach beyond personal and institutional racism. Betty was one person who inspired him, and there were others who taught in the writing program established under the open-enrollment policy at City College. Akmir decided to move out of Harlem for a while. He felt his not-learning had to move him beyond the ghetto. Not-learning made him a discipline problem in school, but ironically it helped him to stay confident as a learner. It prevented him from thinking of himself as a failure or resigning himself to anything less than a fully developed life and self.

In late May of that year things began opening up for Akmir. He had gotten into the open-enrollment program at City College, found a job at Teachers College, and moved into an apartment on the Lower East Side. He began a series of stories about rebirth in what he called his "new language" and was planning a small volume of poetry. In June, however, he got his draft notice, on the same day he received a letter from City College informing him that he needed to show his high school diploma before he could be formally admitted. We visited his high school counselor, and I wrote up a course description and certificate of completion for the psychology course he had taken with Betty and me. The course was to serve as his citizenship class, his atonement for his not-learning in high school. The counselor, to our astonishment, refused to accept the class and told us that he wasn't sure Akmir was repentant enough. He informed us that he would release the diploma at his own pleasure. I pleaded and did everything I could to convince him to change his mind, including trying to use the prestige of Teachers College, where I was a research associate. There was no appeal, though, and we both left the school ready to blow the place up.

As it turned out, Akmir didn't really need the diploma. City College had sent him the wrong letter. But he was devastated by that rejection, fearful of going to jail for being a war resister, and feeling, I believe, that the place he had spent his life clearing was violated or inaccessible. I never saw him alive again. That night, so far as I've been able to reconstruct, Akmir returned to his old neighborhood, ran into some friends, and ended up being abandoned in the emergency room of a nearby hospital where he died of an overdose of heroin—one more victim of what he spent his life not-learning.

Struggling to maintain integrity and hope may not always be the key to survival under conditions of oppression. Imitating your oppressors and trying to integrate yourself into their society might work better. Sometimes survival dictates swallowing one's pride and giving up self-respect. When there is no large-scale movement for liberation, Akmir's alternatives, resistance and rebellion, are lonely and dangerous choices. Some of Akmir's friends became the violent, angry, and dangerous people white society imagined them to be. They succeeded on the streets for a while, but they also set themselves up for eventual self-destruction. Others did what their teachers and bosses told them to do and managed to integrate themselves into certain corners of the white world. Akmir was among those brave people who refused to abandon self-respect or allow himself to be consumed by hatred and self-hatred. Not-learning to think white was a strength that got him in trouble with his teachers, with some of the people he worked for, and with some of his own friends who, as much as they admired his integrity and resistance, felt he was too righteous, too uncompromising. He died pointlessly and in despair, but so far as I'm concerned, his life was honorable and his death a tragic loss.

Over the years, I've come to believe that many of the young people who fail in our schools do so for the same reasons Akmir did and use many of the same strategies he adopted. I remember visiting some teacher friends in San Antonio, Texas, about fifteen years ago. I was there to help them eliminate anti-Latino racism in the public schools in the *barrios*—Latino ghettos. There were very few Latino teachers and no Latino administrators in *barrio* schools in the parts of San Antonio where my friends worked. Many of the administrators were Anglo, retired military personnel from the nearby Randolph Air Force Base who had hostile, imperialist attitudes toward the children they taught and the communities they served. I was asked by a community group, as an outsider and as an Anglo myself, to visit a number of classrooms and participate in some workshops discussing the specific ways in which racism functioned in their schools. In one junior high I was invited to observe a history class by a teacher who admitted that he needed help with this particular group of students, all of whom were Latino. The teacher gave me a copy of his textbook, and I sat in the back of the room and followed the lesson for the day, which was entitled "The First People to Settle Texas." The teacher asked for someone to volunteer to read and no one responded. Most of the students were slumped down in their desks and none of them looked directly at the teacher. Some gazed off into space, others exchanged glimpses and grimaces. The teacher didn't ask for attention but instead started to read the text himself. It went something like, "The first people to settle Texas arrived from New England and the South in . . ." Two boys in the back put their hands in their eyes, there were a few giggles and some murmuring. One hand shot up and that student blurted out, "What are we, animals or something?" The teacher's response was, "What does that have to do with the text?" Then he decided to abandon the lesson, introduced me as a visiting teacher who would substitute for the rest of the period, and left the room. I don't know if he planned to do that all along and set me up to fail with the students just as he did, or if his anger at being observed overcame him and he decided to dump the whole thing on me. Whatever the motivation, he left the room, and I was there with the students. I went up front, reread the sentence from the book, and asked the class to raise their hands if they believed what I had just read. A few of them became alert, though they looked at me suspiciously as I continued, "This is lies, nonsense. In fact, I think the textbook is racist and an insult to everyone in this room." The class woke up, and the same student who had addressed the teacher earlier turned to me and asked, "You mean that?" I said I did, and then he interrupted and said, "Well, there's more than that book that's racist around here."

A few of the other students nodded, and then the class went silent. It was up to me to continue with what I'd opened up or close the conversation down and protect the teacher. I decided to continue on, saying I didn't know their teacher but that I had run into more than one racist who was teaching and ought to be thrown out by the students and their parents. I added that it was obvious that the textbook was racist—the racism was there for everyone to read—but that I wondered how they detected racism in their teachers. The class launched into a serious and sophisticated discussion of the ways racism manifested itself in their everyday lives at school. And they described the stance they took in order to resist that racism and yet not be thrown out of school. It amounted to nothing less than full-blown, cooperative not-learning. They accepted the failing grades not-learning produced in exchange for the passive defense of their personal and cultural integrity. This was a class of school failures, and perhaps, I believed then and still believe, the repository for the positive leadership and intelligence of their generation.

Willed not-learning consists of a conscious and chosen refusal to assent to learn. It manifests itself most often in withdrawal or defiance and is not just a school-related phenomenon. I recently discovered a version of a traditional religious and peace song that goes, "I ain't gonna learn war no more." Learning to make war is the opposite of learning to make peace. Many people who never learned to make war are told they must learn to make war when their nation decides to fight. During those times, pacifists and other people who choose nonviolent ways have to not-learn to make war despite strong social pressures to do so. Poor people have to not-learn despair if they are to survive. Christians have to not-learn pride and arrogance. And on the opposite end of the moral spectrum, soldiers have to not-learn to care about the lives of the "enemy," and the boss has to not-learn to care about the sufferings of fired employees. Throughout life, there may be as much occasion for not-learning as there is occasion for learning. It is uncomfortable to talk about the need to reject certain kinds of learning and reassuring to look at learning in a positive way, but without studying not-learning we can get only a partial view of the complex decisions facing people as they choose values and decide upon actions. I am just beginning to understand the importance of not-learning in the lives of children, and I urge other people to think and write about roads people choose to not-travel and how those choices define character and influence destiny.

In rethinking my teaching experience in the light of not-learning, I realize that many youngsters who ask impertinent questions, listen to their teachers in order to contradict them, and do not take homework or tests seriously are practiced not-learners. The quieter not-learners sit sullenly in class, daydreaming and shutting out the sound of their teacher's voice. They sometimes fall off their chairs or throw things across the room or resort to other strategies of disruption. Some push things so far that they get put in special classes or get thrown out of school. In all of these cases the youngsters' minds are never engaged in learning what the teacher is trying to teach. On that level no failure is possible since there has been no attempt to learn. It is common to consider such students dumb or psychologically disturbed. Conscious, willed refusal of schooling for political or cultural reasons is not acknowledged as an appropriate response to oppressive education. Since students have no way to legitimately criticize the schooling they are subjected to or the people they are required to learn from, resistance and rebellion is stigmatized. The system's problem becomes the victim's problem. However, not-learning is a healthy, though frequently dysfunctional, response to racism, sexism, and other forms of bias. In times of social movements for justice such refusal is often turned to more positive mass protest and demonstration and to the development of alternative learning situations. For example, during the 1960s in New York, students who maintained their integrity and consciously refused the racist teachings of their segregated schools became leaders in school boycotts and teachers of reading and African-American history in Freedom schools.

I've known such student leaders and have had the pleasure of working with some of them. Jamila L., the student-body president of an alternative high school I worked at during the late 1960s, told me that in the regular school she had spent four years in a special-education class drinking orange juice, eating graham crackers, and pretending she couldn't read. The whole act was to keep from hitting several of her teachers who she knew were racist. In fact, she was an avid reader of romances and of black history. She used special education to keep herself in school because her grandmother wanted her to graduate from high school. At our school she was a representative to the school board, helped develop projects and write proposals, and led students in a struggle against racist officers in the juvenile bureau of the local police department.

Jamila was not exceptional. There are many leaders and creators hidden away in the special classes of our schools, running wild in the halls, and hanging out in the bathrooms. In 1967 the poet June Jordan asked me to introduce her to some seniors from Benjamin Franklin High School, which, at that time, was the only high school in Harlem. She was writing an article on what these students planned to do with their futures.* Two of the students were at the bottom of their class and two had done well in school. Jordan described the first two this way:

> Paul Luciano and Victor Hernandez Cruz are friends. Neither of them thinks of graduation, next January, as anything except a time of "getting out" of the school, *per se*. Paul regards the expected "little piece of paper" (the diploma) as proof that you have been "whitey-fied" for four years.

In the course of their conversation Paul says:

> The [school's] program is a very confusing system. There's nobody to explain it to you. They just, you know, like pat you on the back. People tell me if you don't go along with the program, you'll mess up your whole life.
>
> I say then, well, to hell with my life. You have to take some kind of stand. Everything you learn is lies.
> It's their education.   Not mine.
> It's their history.   Not mine.
> It's their language.   Not mine.
> You name it. It's theirs.   Not mine.
>
> A white teacher, he has not lived the life. He cannot relate any of the things to me. So I'm bored.

And Victor goes on a bit later:

> George Washington had slaves, man. You know one time he traded a black man for a pig? . . . We told the librarian we wanted a picture of Malcolm X. We said we would supply our own picture and everything. But she said, "No." We wanted his picture up there with George Washington and Thomas Jefferson . . . the librarian said he preached

---

*Published under the name June Meyer, "You Can't See the Trees for the School." *Urban Review*, vol. 2, no. 3 (December 1967), pp. 11–15.

hate. . . . We asked the librarian to get the *Autobiography of Malcolm X*. She said, "Some books you have to wait three years." It's still not there.

I wonder how many times this situation, so similar to the one portrayed over twenty years later in Spike Lee's movie *Do the Right Thing*, where there is a conflict over putting up pictures of Malcolm X and Martin Luther King next to those of Italian-American heroes in a neighborhood pizza parlor, has to be reenacted?

Later on in Jordan's article it turns out that both Victor and Paul were teaching reading at an education program sponsored by the Citizen's Council of Columbia University, a group that was involved in the student strike at Columbia that year. Both of them wanted to become teachers, the kind of teachers they imagined would empower students. And Victor, in one of his poems quoted in the article, expressed the feeling of most of the young people I have encountered who have chosen the route of not-learning:

> We would not be
> like flowers resting dead in some hill
> not even getting credit for its color
> or the way it smells.

In another poem written that year and published in his first volume of poetry, entitled *Papo Got His Gun*, Victor is much more explicit about the significance of not-learning. In talking about junior high school he writes:

> JHS was boss
> not because of what you taught me
> but because of what I learned
> which was not what you taught me*

---

*Victor Hernandez Cruz, *Papo Got His Gun* (New York: Calle Once Press, 1967), p. 6.

31

Until we learn to distinguish not-learning from failure and to respect the truth behind this massive rejection of schooling by students from poor and oppressed communities, we will not be able to solve the major problems of education in the United States today. Risk taking is at the heart of teaching well. That means that teachers will have to not-learn the ways of loyalty to the system and to speak out, as the traditional African-American song goes, for the concept that everyone has a right to the tree of life. We must give up looking at resistant students as failures and instead turn a critical eye toward this wealthy society and the schools that it supports.

No amount of educational research, no development of techniques or materials, no special programs or compensatory services, no restructuring or retraining of teachers will make any fundamental difference until we concede that for many students the only sane alternative to not-learning is the acknowledgment and direct confrontation of oppression—social, sexual, and economic—both in school and in society. Education built on accepting that hard truth about our society can break through not-learning and can lead students and teachers together, not to the solution of problems but to direct intelligent engagement in the struggles that might lead to solutions.

The Tattooed Man
Confessions of a Hopemonger

IT WAS IN November or December of 1949, in the early after-noon, about one-thirty or two, just when the grey Bronx dusk of early winter reminded me that asthma was only a few hours away. My afternoons those days were overpowered by fear of an attack, the same fear that brought on the attacks. Seventh-graders had to go to the library for a lesson on the Dewey decimal system. We all followed along, paying no attention to Mr. Robertson, who was probably drunk as usual. He wasn't in a rush either—going to the library meant one less teaching period for him.

The librarian went on about numbers and indexes, and talked about how wonderful reading was, or something. I was lost studying the nuances of my anxiety, wondering why it was worse this time of year, so bad sometimes that I almost cried on the way home from school. Those days anxiety and asthma settled around me like river fog, and I had no language or concepts to under-stand them.

Our assignment was to find a book, any book, return to our places at one of the tables, and fill out the Dewey decimal num-ber, title, author, and some other information. Another walk-through assignment. I went to a shelf in the farthest corner of the

33

room and picked a book at random: *The Tattooed Man* by Howard Pease, an intriguing title stolen from my dreams and an author whose name was foreign and mysterious, not Jewish or Irish or Italian, but what? Where do people get such names? Pease and the tattooed man were equally intriguing. I knew tattooed men and masked men and invisible people. I read the subtitle, *A Tale of Strange Adventures Befalling Tod Moran, Mess Boy of the Tramp Steamer "Araby," Upon His First Voyage from San Francisco to Genoa, via the Panama Canal,* thinking of my own fantasies and dreams, my personal twists on the heroes and heroines that I followed on radio and in comic books.

My attention wandered back to the table, to Dewey decimal numbers, only instead of filling out the work sheet I wrote down the book's dedication "For Guard C. Darrah: This memory of rain-swept decks off Panama and the marching roads of France," feeling the rain, thinking how sweet it must be to be wandering, wondering about marching roads and rain-swept decks. I never finished the assignment and to this day have resisted learning how the Dewey decimal system works.

There have only been a few times in my life when I was certain that a book was positioned in a library or bookstore for the sole purpose of my discovering it. This was one. I never begged a librarian to borrow a book before that day, but succeeded in getting *The Tattooed Man* loaned to me for two weeks though students were not allowed to check out books and take them home. That was barely enough time, for I've never been able to read a book that I loved quickly. My style is to linger over the words, question the text, stop reading when my mind is full or when I want time to understand the ideas, guess the writer's next trick, or anticipate the characters' next responses.

That night after homework I picked up the book and joined Tod Moran in San Francisco, where "sea fog hazed like spindrift along the San Francisco waterfront." I couldn't figure out what

34

spindrift was from the context, and only recently looked up its meaning. The word feels right to me when I think of Tod Moran and remember that night when I was drawn into his world and traveled with him to a city smothered in mist, listening with him to "the distant clang of cable cars, the hoar crys of newsboys, the dull rumble of trucks and drays passing in the gloom like ghosts." That sentence stopped me. I read it over, then over again, and spoke it out loud, quietly so my parents and brother couldn't hear. It conjured up a picture in my mind that was more intense than most of my dreams. Howard Pease's words created a world; they were magic and set me on fire with a burning desire to become a writer.

Since that night the necessity of writing has never left me. I still can't explain how or why it happened and often wonder whether the need to write was always in me waiting for some—any—beautiful words to activate it or whether, if my junior high school librarian had not decided to acquire a copy of *The Tattooed Man*, I would still be waiting to be inspired.

I was twelve, San Francisco was a dot on the map of the United States, and drays and cable cars were unreal vehicles contiguous with the horses and submarines of my dream adventures. Only Tod Moran was not like my dream companions. He had a real brother who had mysteriously disappeared at sea. On a ship called the *Araby* he met a tattooed man who knew of his brother. And Tod knew that he, the younger brother, had to find and redeem his older brother. This was not the stuff of comic book dreams. It was reality, the reality of literature, more dimensional, deeper, and more moving than anything I had encountered in comic books.

Tod Moran went to sea and he wasn't even seventeen. That meant only five years for me to wait. When, on page 20, I learned that Tod got a job as mess boy on the *Araby*, I stopped reading for five days and thought about my future, which had suddenly become real to me and not merely composed of heroic fantasies and halfhearted plots to run away from home. I began to think of the actual world as bigger, more variable, and more accessible than I had imagined and realized that I too could change my life and live in different ways and in different places. My imaginings didn't have to be confined to unreal and unrealizable domains.

From the time I was about eight until I was twelve, I often put myself to sleep with guided fantasies of romance and adventure. These fantasies never intruded upon my daytime existence and were called forth by a specific ritual. First tuck under the bedcovers; next turn on my back and look up at the ceiling for the reflection of the Lexington Avenue elevated subway.

On Jerome Avenue the subway was elevated several stories above ground. The apparent contradiction between being elevated and underground was resolved for me every weekend when on my trip to Manhattan I stood at the window of the front car of the train and experienced its plunge underground at the station past Yankee Stadium. At that moment the lights went out, and the dark interior of the train became one with the darkness of the tunnel. I imagined, and I know my friends also imagined, demons and dybbuks and spirits unleashed on the train for that forty-five seconds that the whole world was dark. When I was about thirteen, I thought of writing a science fiction story about a train from the Bronx to Manhattan that became suspended in time the moment it went underground.

The el was part of my thinking as well as part of my nighttime ritual. It was a metaphor of passage, from the Bronx to Manhattan, and from daytime into my nighttime adventures and fantasies. Once I was in the right position to see the el's reflection on my bedroom wall, I had to wait. The third part of my ritual couldn't begin until I heard the train leave the 176th Street station and saw the lights reflected by each of the train windows pass over my bed, sometimes outlined so distinctly that I could make out the silhouettes of the people sitting at each window. After the magic lights had passed, I closed my eyes and called forth my fantasy companion and teacher, the Masked Rider. Sometimes he immediately appeared in dream time and I was already there with him. Other times he was waiting and it seemed as if I walked into the dream and joined him.

I have tried to reconstruct some of the feelings of that experience, and remember that the Masked Rider was faceless and rode a dark horse. He was friendly, very skillful with weapons, but non-violent, and had many adventures during the three or four years he was willing to come when I summoned him. I was his companion, and on particularly good nights I experienced myself stepping into my dream or fantasy and asking him where we were going that night. Most of our adventures involved a sweet, accepting young woman who could like you without controlling you. I'm not sure that I was aware that my dreams were experiments with love outside the family, but in retrospect they were preparing me for leaving home spiritually as well as physically.

I remember somehow knowing about the Masked Rider's past, though he never explicitly talked about it. He was found as a child wandering across a vast plain wearing a dark mask. No one was bold enough to unmask him and he never showed his face to anyone. He had never even seen his own face. He lived on a dark edge of the world, alone with a bundle of sacred objects, a sword, and a rope. He had stones that resembled faces, a root that was a clenched fist, four beautiful steel knives, a few empty jars, and a vial of black sand. The most sacred object was a small clay head worn featureless by time, a faceless relic the Masked Rider found when he was a child. He sometimes rode a black, feature-less horse. At those times they were one, horse-and-rider, all in black.

During the day I listened to *Captain Midnight* on the radio. I also listened to *The Shadow, The Lone Ranger,* and *The Thin Man.*

The Masked Rider was my personal reconstruction of the freedom and power these programs represented for me. My encounters with the Masked Rider were not like other dreams over which I had no control. I was both in a fantasy world and semiawake outside of that world, aware of what was going on. I could at times experience the adventures we had together and at other times witness my own adventures. I could even give advice to the me in the dream, and somehow in dream logic it made sense for me to exist on both planes simultaneously, within and outside the fantasy. My double and I lived through all of those adventures together.

During our adventures the Masked Rider rescued the young, nurtured them for their own sake, and left them to grow strong. And he showed me how to be caring and tough at the same time. There are times when I've wondered whether the dream of being a teacher of young children, which I've nurtured since I was twelve or thirteen, isn't intimately connected with my admiration for the Masked Rider and my desire to be as nurturing to others as he was to me.

I never told anyone about the Masked Rider, for two reasons. First, I was afraid he would disappear; and second, I was afraid people would think I was crazy.

With both *The Tattooed Man* and the Masked Rider, I was learning to move through and beyond the world as I knew it and imagine other, more congenial and exciting possibilities. Over the years, I've also encouraged my students to learn how to dream beyond the world they lived in and imagine ways in which life can be made fuller and more compassionate. The ability to see the world as other than it is plays a major role in sustaining hope. It keeps part of one's mind free of the burden of everyday misery and can become a corner of sanity as one struggles to undo the horrors of an unkind and mad world.

Nurturing children's ability to imagine ways in which the

world might be different is a gift we owe all children. This can be done in many ways. Telling children stories, for example, allows them to enter worlds where the constraints of ordinary life are transcended. The phrase "enter into" is not merely a metaphor: children step into good stories, just as I stepped into the world of the Masked Rider, and listen as if in a trance. Phrases like "Once upon a time" or "Long ago in a land far away" are ritualistic ways of informing children that reality is being suspended and fantasy taking over. When I've taught kindergarten, story time was sacred. If someone came in and interrupted an absorbing story, the children would look up as if awakened from a dream and would often chase intruders away. It seemed as if a violation of their inner space had occurred, some involuntary awakening from another world.

Those times I've taught high school, poetry has been my vehicle for honoring the imagination. The legitimate breaking of the bonds of factuality offered by poetry has helped me overcome adolescent cynicism about the power of fairy tales and myths.

I remember making up stories and telling them to my three children when they were young. The stories I had heard from my grandparents at their ages didn't seem right for my children. The stories I wanted to tell involved the children themselves or at least surrogate characters who represented them. The stories revolved around four characters. Three—Mimi, Tutu, and Jha—were modeled on the children: Mimi on Erica, who was six at the time; Tutu on Tonia, who was seven; and Jha on Joshua, who was four. The fourth character was called Overall. He lived underground in a worldwide network of sewers that went under oceans, deserts, and mountains as well as cities. He appeared as steam and spoke with a Yiddish accent. He was, for me, a representation of all the humor, bitterness, rage, gentleness, roughness, and intelligence of the Yiddish world of my grandparents and of the Bronx I knew as a child. He may also have been an embodiment of the asthmatic fog that was both suffocating and nurturing during my Bronx childhood.

Overall was my way of trying to share with my children, in a story setting, the flavor and spirit of a part of their inheritance they could never directly experience. Overall had one peculiar power that figured in all of the stories I made up over the three or four years that the stories continued: whenever and wherever there was real trouble for the three young adventurers, a manhole cover appeared on the ground and Overall steamed up through the holes in the cover, coming to the rescue.

Overall also presented each of the children with a present: detached eyeballs that they could carry around and use to see things they wished to see. They could look into the eyeballs and see distant places, could plant the eyeballs in places where they wanted to spy on what was going on, and could even see into the past and sometimes the future. In the case of the future, however, the eyeballs became teary and the images were cloudy and indefinite so that future vision was unreliable.

The eyeballs were only part of the powers I, as storyteller, granted Mimi, Tutu, and Jha. Erica is a Capricorn, so she, Mimi, got the power to climb the steepest hills and to butt through the hardest materials, and the ability to solve riddles. Tonia is a Cancer, so Tutu had the power of moving sideways as quickly as forward or backward, of grabbing on to things and not letting go until she got what she wanted, and of having immense patience and the ability to think through complex problems and come up with interesting solutions. Joshua is a Scorpio, so Jha had the power of sudden stinging attack, the ability to make caves and tunnels underground, and a sharp intellect that let him understand other people's thoughts and feelings.

Each story began as a simple voyage on a ship in mid-ocean or in the middle of a forest or the depths of a city like New York. I would set the scene and then ask the children where they wanted to go. They helped me spin out the story and teased out of me all kinds of enemies and friends, characters to people the story world. I always kept Overall for particularly difficult times, and always gave him a story or two to tell, one that was directly set in the Bronx where I grew up, and obliquely related to the situation. They had to be patient, to learn his ways of teaching by story-telling. As the tales grew in complexity and the children demanded I remember details and take up a telling at exactly the point it was dropped, I realized the importance of our half hour or hour together. I could introduce them to what I remembered and loved about my growing up through the character of Overall. They could frame adventures out of their fears and anxieties. We could embark on adventures and voyages together, and our imaginations played with the possible. As long as none of the characters was killed, we could go on indefinitely imagining worlds and testing powers. I was drawn into the tales even on days when I felt no stories in me. The children provided the energy for the telling and remembered all of the little details that made the world come alive. At times when my imagination failed, they also took up the telling and contributed to the making of that alternate world.

Even now, more than fifteen years later, with the details of all of the stories forgotten, Overall is alive for all of the children, as are Mimi, Tutu, and Jha. The circle within which the tales were created was magical in a way. The children could experiment with being strong; I could memorialize my grandparents and pass something on of their world. In addition, the four of us could enter a world of the possible and keep alive the idea that the world did not have to be the way it was and that we could exercise powers that could lead to its transformation.

I also try to tell empowering stories when I teach, and I encourage students to create their own tales and imaginings. In periods of stress, when people don't take the time to tell or listen to stories, they sacrifice their imaginations and allow hope to slip away. I've never had any problem trading formal learning for story-telling in my classes, and I believe the students have been richer for it. After all, seeding hope is at the center of the art and craft of teaching.

Creating hope in oneself as a teacher and nourishing or rekin-dling it in one's students is the central issue educators face today. After thirty years of teaching, trying to reform public schools, and continuing to work in a framework of hope, I have had to exam-ine the sources of my own hope and my struggles with the temp-tation to despair and quit. They go back to the Bronx, to the Masked Rider and the Tattooed Man. They also go back to adults who passed through my life those days in the way poems do now—as sources of images that tutor my sensibility and tease my usual ways of looking at the world into new images of the possible.

I remember an old man who walked through our neighbor-hood two or three times a week crying, "I buy old clothes." I must have been seven or eight at the time. He had a sack of rags tied into a bundle strapped to his back, and I remember thinking he was a hunchback with magical powers. Over the years I've built up memories of him and stories about his life, though I have no way of knowing how much my image resembles the man him-self or his life. For me he has a high-pitched voice, a long thin nose, and very dirty though sensitive hands.

He wasn't the only peddler in the neighborhood, but other than the scissors- and knife-sharpening man who carried his grinder on his back, he was the only one on foot. There was an ice man with a tired horse that the old people used to joke about, an Italian fruit and vegetable man with a horse-drawn wagon that smelled of apples, peaches, onions, and fresh soil. There was also the egg and butter man who was modern and carried his produce from upstate to the Bronx in the back of his station wagon.

The "I buy old clothes" man was my favorite. I liked to follow him close enough to talk with him if I dared. Other kids followed him at a distance and made fun of him. They were afraid to get too close since he was our bogey man, the person who, the grown-ups told us, always knew what you were doing and had curses that could cause harm at unexpected moments. The people in my parents' generation both demonized him and were ashamed of him. He was one of us—a Jew—but too Old World, too poor, too unashamed of his peddling. He was not a good model, in our parents' minds, for we were to be a generation headed out of the ghetto to college and the professions.

I was scared of him too, but also loved him because the scorn, disdain, mockery, and foolishness he encountered didn't seem to bother him at all. He had secrets that I wanted to know and, scared as I was, I was determined to talk to him. I don't know if I ever did, but at some point during my adolescence I constructed a short exchange we might have had, one which has stuck in my memory. I told him I knew what he was buying, but that I wondered if he was also selling something, and his response was, "Hope, I'm selling hope."

He was a hopemonger. I have never forgotten that—hope can be sold, it can be taught or at least spread, it can survive in the strangest and most unlikely places. It is a force that does not disappear. I keep that idea as a counter to the cynicism of reality-mongers, who try to sell the idea that compassion is a form of weakness and hope and justice are illusions. It is a guiding principle of my teaching and writing, one that provides the moral grounds of the struggles I have been involved in over the past thirty years.

The image of myself as an "I buy old clothes" teacher, a monger of hope, still delights me. One of my fantasies during the 1970s was to send hobo reading teachers across the country to help solve the problem of illiteracy and make themselves available to help eliminate poverty. These teachers would set themselves up on the streets, in parks, on basketball courts, in marketplaces, in front of schools, and offer reading lessons and writing services while they mongered hope.

Thinking about education and learning outside of the context of formal institutions and the way they define people is central to the ability to see the strengths in people and look beyond their failures and despair. This is particularly true when trying to understand what children might become if the world were a more decent place. Looking at a child, understanding something of who she or he is or might become, is not a simple neutral act or a matter of finding the right objective test or experimental situation. Central to what you see in someone is what you are looking for. If you want to find a child's weaknesses, failures, personal problems, or inadequacies, you'll discover them. If you look at a child through the filter of her or his environment or economic status, and make judgments through the filters of your own cultural, gender, and racial biases, you'll find the characteristics you expect. You'll also find yourself well placed to reproduce failure and to develop resistance in some children, a false sense of superiority in others. On the other hand, if you look for strengths and filter the world through the prism of hope, you will see and encourage the unexpected flowering of child life in the most unlikely places.

Hope makes it possible for children to become active creators of their own values. It allows them to experiment with the consequences of moral choice. As early as five, children have ways of countering and overriding reality, of entertaining ideas, values, and ways of living that go beyond what they experience. In other words, by the age of five, children encounter the possibility of choice and the ability to make themselves—that is, to create ways of being in the world that differ from those of their parents, friends—and the culture, rather than being fully made by the world they are born into. It is this ability to imagine the world as other than it is that leads to hope and the belief that even the most oppressive and difficult of conditions are not absolute.

When I was teaching in a one-room schoolhouse about six years ago, Karen, one of my kindergarten students, showed me the power of hope and the imaginary worlds it generates in young lives. In April she took to running away from school just before it was time for her to go home during our lunch break. She lived near the school and would sneak past her house and, as soon as she was sure her mother wasn't watching, would take off running down the street. For several days I would have to drop everything, follow her, and carry her back to the school, where her mother was waiting to pick her up. It was difficult to persuade her to walk back with me, and I had the unpleasant task of having to pick her up and carry her, crying and kicking, to the lot next to the school, where I put her down and let her compose herself before taking her hand and leading her back to school.

After this happened a few times, I talked to Karen during the morning and tried to discover a way to prevent the runaway ritual. She refused to talk, but I did find out that her mother had just broken up with her boyfriend and was in a continual bad mood. Karen had reason to want to leave home, but she and her mother also had a close and warm relationship that had survived hard times before. Pretending to run away was her way of envisioning a better life and acting out her imagined reconstruction of reality. I decided to talk to Karen's mom and provide help to deal with the situation. I knew the mother and was sure she and Karen would be fine together when her anger and grieving subsided. Karen wasn't abused, and my feeling was that it was better for the two of them to weather that particular storm together than for me to bring in a public agency or third party.

One afternoon, after a morning talk about running away, Karen came up to me and handed me the following drawing:

Then she told me the story behind the drawing. She said she was going to go off and live in the woods by herself. She would build a wagon that could carry her house and would get people to help her put the house on the wagon when her mother wasn't home.

She said she was going to put her dog in the house and pull the wagon into the woods where she and the dog could live happily and without violence. She imagined her world intact, in the woods, full of peace and kindness. Her mother, she said, would have to build a new house.

That day she didn't run away. She said her plan, her drawing, and the world she imagined in the woods was on her mind, and she drew pictures of the woods and of her house in the woods. I suggested she share the drawing and idea with her mother, who by this time was calm enough to discuss with Karen the tension in their lives. It was moving for Theresa, the mother, to find that Karen loved the house so much even though she couldn't stand what was happening inside of it. It also showed her how pained Karen was by the personal turmoil that surrounded her, and created an opening for them to talk about ways of putting their lives together. Five-year-olds are not beyond such confidences and responsibility.

Karen's imaginary journey into the woods reminded me of my adventures with the Masked Rider. My dream teacher rescued the young, nurtured them for their own sake, and left them to grow strong. There are times when I've wondered whether the idea of being a teacher of young children isn't intimately connected with my admiration for the Masked Rider and my desire to be as nurturing to others as he was to me. I know that encountering new children, a new class or school, has been an adventure to me that is more exciting and challenging than almost all of the actual physical voyages I've ever taken.

When I was eleven or twelve, the Masked Rider disappeared, and all-night reading sessions with the complete writings of Howard Pease took their place. *The Tattooed Man* wasn't enough for me, and I made my way through *Jinx Ship, Heart of Danger, Shanghai Passage*, and other Pease books I can't recall. I never spoke to anyone about the books, never used them for library or school book reports. Reading them, sometimes two or three times, became an intimate necessity, not something to share but to take in and center in my memory. I loved them as story and studied them as writing. While reading those books, it dawned on me

47

that people make books and that ordinary people like me could do it. This may sound trivial, but no one in my family had ever published anything or aspired to write, as far as I knew. The few times I mentioned my interest in writing, I was told that it would be a good hobby but that I should study hard and get on with learning a profession. My parents and grandparents wanted me to acquire skills they imagined would make me immune from future depressions.

Anxiety and abiding sadness afflicted the whole neighborhood those days. Though the end of World War II was a joy for most Americans, in the working-class Jewish neighborhood I grew up in, it was a time of misery, suspicion, and more war. People were searching for relatives in displaced-persons camps, waiting and often receiving news about who died in the concentration camps, and thinking about participating in the war to create a Jewish state in Palestine. My next-door neighbor came home from fighting the war in Europe only to leave for Palestine a few months later. His death was yet another cause of grief, though he became a hero to many of my friends. Even after World War II ended, my friends and I continued playing the war games we invented in the early 1940s, only now the enemy was the British.

McCarthyism and red baiting added another bitter spice to the flavor of life in the Bronx in the late forties and early fifties. My parents and their friends had either been members of the Communist Party or were sympathetic to socialist or Communist ideas during the Depression. By 1950 they found themselves under siege, losing jobs, afraid for their children's ability to get into college, uncertain about how far the FBI and the government would go to persecute them or destroy their family lives. At the very time they began to experience prosperity in their small businesses or win decent wages in the unions, they found themselves enemies of the state that they believed would protect them as they made their way out of marginality.

My parents, and the parents of many of my friends, tried to protect their children from the threats of red baiting and the sorrows of discovering who was dead and who was lost somewhere in a camp waiting for a place to go. As a ten-year-old, I knew vaguely about the problems that made my parents and their friends sad and bitter, and I knew how the struggle in Palestine was the one small hope in many of their lives. But in my family the rule was not to talk about adult problems in front of the children. What filtered through to me was the anxiety and uncertainty, the just barely contained rage at the concentration camps and the red baiting, and the fear that the United States might abandon its Jews just as it had abandoned the Jews in Europe during the thirties. And because so much was left unspoken, I felt that I was partially responsible for the dejection of all of the adults around me. My asthma and anxiety were intensified by this vague sense that I was in complicity with all of the forces that worked against my parents' and grandparents' happiness.

By the time I was in high school, however, I began to understand some of the pressure they were under and vowed never to hide my feelings from my own children, something much harder to do than I imagined in those days. I didn't want my children to suffer the undefined anxiety that led me to the Masked Rider, to fantasies of running away from home, and to a sense of guilt whenever I was enjoying myself. This sense that unadulterated joy should be a cause of guilt is still with me, though as far back as I can remember, I've been able to build a small wall around myself and take joy within its protection.

The Masked Rider fantasies protected my freedom, but I was unable to fend off the feeling that some important parts of me were being smothered in the house I lived in. These feelings were particularly intense during asthma attacks. One night stands out even now. I awoke with a severe asthma attack from a dream of losing the Masked Rider, of his telling me that he had to go away

49

for a while on some adventures that were too hard for me. My parents rushed to my bedroom and gave me some medicine, the strong kind that relieved major attacks but left me exhausted and jumpy for a day or two. Then they insisted I lie down in bed between them until the attack receded. My suffocation was suffocated by my parents' overweening kindness. Their love for me and their anxiety over my breathing and wheezing was terrifying.

Of course everything wasn't grim those days. I was a member of a modestly successful comic-book theft ring, belonged to a secret club that ventured into Manhattan on Saturdays and explored Macy's, Gimbels, and the Gilbert Hall of Science the way rural kids probably explored the woods. I became friendly with a woman who played popular hits and sold sheet music at Macy's. She taught me how to play the melody line of sheet music on her grand piano. I also took free chess lessons in the adult games department. My friends Jules and Leon taught me how to steal semivaluable postage stamps from the stamp department of Gimbels. I loved to spend hours in those department stores learning from all of the wonderful people who were hired to demonstrate and sell things I knew my parents either couldn't afford or would never bring into our house. I particularly loved the book, game, and toy departments and came to know many of the salespeople on a first-name basis. I was allowed to try out almost anything as long as there were no customers around.

Those experiences overcame my boredom with school and taught me how to find real teachers and places of learning, the first time it occurred to me that I might be able to take conscious control over my own education. To this day my favorite sources of educational and writing ideas are bookstores, toy stores, and department stores. I learned early on not to mistake schooling for learning, which takes place out of school at least as much as it does within it.

At home I learned from my grandparents and their friends, none of whom had any formal schooling. They told stories, talked about union politics, the horrors of the old country, and the latest in Yiddish theater. Central to their life was the struggle for working people's right to decent lives. My grandparents were active in the Workmen's Circle and in union activities. Their passion and willingness to take risks and confront oppressive conditions showed me the dignity and power of saying "I won't," of refusing to conform when conforming meant tolerating injustice. From them I learned not to mistake schooling for intelligence or honesty.

A great-uncle of mine, Julius Malamud, was the first teacher who inspired me with the wonder of helping other people grow strong. Uncle Julius had been a member of the Vienna Opera chorus as a child and was a gymnasium student in his native Vienna before the First World War. As a young Jew involved in radical politics around 1918, he was not safe in Vienna and fled to the United States. There he became a waiter and was involved in the formation of the Hotel Employees and Restaurant Employees Union. When I was about eleven or twelve, I used to visit with Julius occasionally on Saturdays after my accordion lessons.

Those days Julius was a waiter in a small Jewish delicatessen on Madison Avenue around Twenty-fourth Street in Manhattan. I remember his work uniform—black pants, a black string bow tie, white shirt, black vest, and a clean white towel folded over one of his arms. He was almost formally dressed, suited, I used to think, for going to the opera he loved so much.

My lessons with Julius took place between customers, interrupted by his carrying pastrami and corned-beef sandwiches to his tables, tallying checks, or exchanging union gossip with customers. I sat in the back room of the deli, next to his phonograph machine, listening to the music he had set aside for me. One week it was *La Boheme*, another it was Paul Robeson singing Earl Robinson's *Ballad for Americans*. When he had a minute, he paused and talked with me about the social and artistic significance of the music—about the life of an artist in Paris or the importance of blacks and whites coming together to struggle for social and economic justice. He gave me a copy of Max Eastman's condensation of Karl Marx's *Capital*, which we discussed. He taught me to play chess and to think chess. In what I first took to be a hit-or-miss way, he undertook my intellectual, social, and political education. Only when I became a teacher myself did I understood how important it is to introduce resources to your students, to cross subject and theme boundaries, and to relate everything that is learned to a moral and social purpose.

Julius showed me the joy of learning and the central role of trust on the part of the learner. He welcomed me to master what he knew and to grow beyond it too. Later in his life, after I had been teaching and writing for a while, he told me how proud he was of me because I took the things he showed me and, as a teacher, shared them with others.

I never spoke to anyone about my meetings with Julius just as I never spoke to anybody about Howard Pease's novels—they were my special secret and inspiration. But when I got my first opportunity to teach someone else, I jumped at it. It came during my first year in high school. My chemistry teacher, Mr. Klinesinger, took me aside one day and asked me if I would like to teach his son how to read. Teaching was a gift I admired, and, since my experiences with Julius, I had thought about teaching, though not necessarily about becoming a schoolteacher.

Still, when Mr. Kleinsinger asked me to teach his son, Robert, I was more frightened than flattered. I had no idea how to teach reading and even less of a sense of why he chose me, but I accepted. To my surprise, Robert was a year older than I was and could already read. In fact, he had read more widely and deeply than I had. However, Robert had severe cerebral palsy, never left his apartment, and didn't have any friends. My first teaching experience was as a companion, friend, and fellow learner. I don't know if our time together was useful to Robert, but it set forces and energy loose in me that have played a central role in my development. I am still trying to understand the character of those forces and the source of that energy. As I try to reconstruct our times together over forty years ago, what stands forth are Robert's struggles to communicate ideas, feelings, and thoughts that were clear to him but which his physical and physiological self distorted into grunts and groans and gestures. Watching his face and feeling the intense intelligence projected through his eyes, it was clear that what sounded incoherent to me was in fact a new language I had to, and eventually did, learn.

Spending time with Robert taught me how to look beyond gesture and sound, beyond style and form, into something deeper within a person that revealed strengths and dreams that the surface concealed. It also taught me about courage and persistence. Robert was very funny and very kind. He had patience with my lack of ease around him. After a while I learned to laugh at his jokes about himself and about the people who mistook his palsy for retardation. We became close, part of each other's world.

I learned many things from him, since he had taken the time to read and reflect about his reading and was eager to share his insights and questions. But what did I teach him? What in our relationship released the teacher in me? I believe it was the pleasure I got from helping him reach out to me and through that experience learn ways of reaching out to other people. I could feel him getting more hopeful about having a place in the world with other people, of being liked, and being of use. His humor was often bitter and self-deprecating, but it became less so. He learned to joke about the world and talk about what he could give others. Receiving help all the time was a burden to him, and the thought that he too could be a giving person was a new source of joy for him.

Our relationship revealed to me that people could strengthen each other and keep alive dreams of a better world on a personal and intimate level, even in difficult political and social times. It implied that it was possible to get beyond stigma and ego, and was a seed of my conviction that a wonderful way to spend one's life is peddling hope in the face of despair and cynicism. This has sustained my work and thinking over the past forty years.

As an adolescent, especially before I went to the Bronx High School of Science, I experienced other noneducational political pressures. The gangs hit my neighborhood in the early 1940s. Though the streets were only mildly attractive to me, I tried to adjust to the glamour of gang life and kept a black Ike jacket, combat boots, and a switchblade knife hidden in the basement of a friend's house. When I was in junior high, I wore that uniform on weekends—out of sight of my parents and relatives, of course. All of my friends did the same thing and most seemed to enjoy it. I felt then, as I've felt most of my life, both part of and apart from the world I lived in. Dressing like a gang member was theater—not a sign of my toughness so much as proof that I wanted to be on stage with everyone else, to be part of the cast even though the play itself frightened and repulsed me.

Once, when I was in junior high school, my friends and I were hanging out on the corner of University and Tremont avenues. There was talk of a rumble in the air, and Italian and Irish gangs from my neighborhood were posturing and menacing the Puerto Rican and black gangs that were coming uptown to the Bronx from Harlem. This was in 1949, and the paraphernalia of gang warfare was army surplus. My friends and I ran into a Puerto Rican gang—or rather we were hanging out on the corner and seven guys got off the bus, saw us, and asked us if we were ready to fight. I remember one of them looked at me—sensing my lack of conviction and experience, I'm sure—and announced that I was his. He then engaged me in a staring contest. I looked straight at him, refusing to look away for what seemed like a long time, and then looked away. Without a word or a blow, he had won. My friends postured a bit more, but we ended up beating a complete and somewhat undignified retreat from the corner we had claimed. Later in the year, with the exception of George and Jan, we abandoned our Ike jackets, boots, and faux gang. I kept my switchblade and hid it in my bedroom. George and Jan joined with the Italians.

I was delighted to have lost with dignity. It freed me. Now I didn't have to pretend I could fight. I didn't have to say yes to being strong in ways I didn't want to be. And most of all I learned how to not fight battles I didn't care to win or be pushed into public competition for the sake of someone else's sense of the importance of winning.

By the time I was ten, I felt that I needed to leave my family and the Bronx and all of the ways of the streets and begin again to create a sweeter, simpler world. My fantasies were full of hints of trees, glimpses of clouds, the sounds of flowing water, and the presence of people who didn't hurt all of the time. There were many times as a child when I felt that the only way I could be affirmative and feel positive about life was by running away—but I never did.

I held on to the Masked Rider as long as I could, but with the coming of adolescence the Rider wandered out of my dreams. About that time I discovered Tod Moran and *The Tattooed Man*. My encounter with Tod Moran, though it was qualitatively different than the one with the Masked Rider, had the same intimacy and urgency. Tod's first night out at sea felt like my first voyage away from home, and I still get chills when I reread Howard Pease's introduction to the voyage of the *Araby* in *The Tattooed Man*.

> How little he [Tod] . . . knew that morning of the ways of ocean tramps! Unlike the great passenger greyhounds that ply regularly across the lanes of the sea as promptly as the overland express trains, the tramp freighter, rusty and woebegone of aspect, comes and goes like a will-o'-the wisp, sailing days and even weeks after its scheduled departure. It follows not the well-charted lanes of travel, but takes to the open sea, filling its holds with cargo disdained by the larger ships, and taking it to remote ports of the world seldom visited by its luxurious sisters.
>
> The crews, too, are men of a different stamp. Their seamanship has been learned before the mast, in the rigging of windjammers rounding the Horn, where life is cheap and the food sea biscuits and salt horse. They know the far ports of the world as a cockney knows the streets of London; they look with contempt upon those well-fed seamen who are familiar only with their regular ports of call.*

I knew the world of a tramp steamer the moment I read those words, knew the ship not as a mere fantasy like the Masked Rider but as reality that could be touched through books. I discovered that reading fiction was a way into worlds that were not constructed by me, nor sprung from my needs and fantasies. It provided an external palette to experiment with, one that took me beyond anything I had experienced or felt. I didn't live vicariously through the fiction, want, for example, to be Tod Moran or take to sea on a tramp steamer. I took *The Tattooed Man* and other fiction I began to read as part survival manual, part psychology and sociology textbook, part metaphor for different journeys I would take one day, and part travelogue.

---

*Howard Pease, *The Tattooed Man* (Garden City, NY: Doubleday, 1946), p. 37.

After reading *The Tattooed Man*, I felt I lived in a larger world. It wasn't that I intended to take to sea but that it was clear that the world was not the Bronx and that it was possible to get out and move on. People who have never lived in ghettos may have a hard time understanding one of the main features of ghetto life: the world becomes the ghetto. Its problems and pleasures, its politics and variety, become the palette that colors and limits your thinking. After encountering Tod Moran, I began dreaming of California—and of creating written worlds that were not like the ones I knew.

That did not mean that I intended to abandon my family and community entirely. Rather, it meant that I had to change my relationship to it, see it from outside, and get in touch with that part of myself that was free from the stigmas created by exclusion and anti-Semitism. It meant becoming more in control of how I lived and being open to what could be learned from people outside of the ghetto, people with different ideals, dreams, and values that I needed to encounter. It meant setting the world I grew up in as a child in the context of the larger world that both defined our Bronx ghetto and promised riches we never imagined.

My uncle Julius introduced me to opera, and in high school I was introduced to symphonic and chamber music—in particular, Mozart's. His music was a revelation. I had never heard such music until I was a junior in high school, and Mozart's string quartets and piano concertos brought me unanticipated and almost overwhelming joy. I wasn't the only one who felt this way. A friend, Ralph Lehman, was in the music class and seemed equally moved. The two of us talked a lot about music, mathematics, and ideas those days. We also took wandering tours around Manhattan's old bookstores and museums on weekends. One Saturday we decided to see what Fifty-seventh Street was like. Uptown Manhattan from about Fifty-seventh Street to Ninety-sixth Street was unknown territory to me then. Ralph and I passed Carnegie Hall, which I had never heard of, and noticed an announcement for a concert by the New York Philharmonic with the pianist Paul Badura-Skoda. Badura-Skoda was playing Mozart's twenty-seventh piano concerto. My first thought was, "Oh my god, they're playing Mozart in New York this year," and I found a way to get a ticket during the next week. I was afraid that if I didn't it would be several years before there would be another public performance of Mozart's music in New York, and I would miss a unique opportunity.

Live music, and especially that particular concert, was beautiful beyond all expectation. I might even call that experience life-transforming, in that music, all kinds of music I never knew of as a child, has become an abiding joy in my life. It is hard for many people to realize that what is ordinary for them, a matter of common experience, can be a revelation to other people. Throughout my teaching life my first encounter with live Mozart has been a metaphor for the joy of discovering that the world is larger and more beautiful than you imagined it. It has allowed me to explore new subjects and themes over the years, to move from a Bronx-centric stance in the world to one that is open to experiencing the range and variety of human creations that make life complex and so confoundingly challenging. It has also allowed me to understand that not knowing something is no crime if one never had an opportunity to know it. I refuse to judge students on the basis of what they can't do or don't know. Rather, one of my roles as a teacher is to insinuate complexity into the lives of my students, to present them with new experiences and ideas whether they be contemporary or ancient, local or global. I know I could not have invented Mozart myself, and contrary to some educators who would have us believe that children create their own worlds, I know that worlds created by individuals are tiny and that children need to connect with culture and history as much as they need to be free to contribute to them. Fear of multiculturalism, of learning things that force you to change the way you view the world, is akin to putting down my encounter with Mozart as a betrayal of the Bronx.

Over the years, I have had a number of significant encounters with literature. In high school I graduated from Tod Moran to Stephen Dedalus. Dedalus traveled in the world of ideas, elevated literature to a central part of his soul, and had the same longings I had to know more about things that were not around me. I had moved beyond dreaming of voyaging on a tramp steamer to dreaming of books I would write about adventures I had not yet experienced. In my junior and senior years in high school, I sat at my grandparents' kitchen table holding a pen and facing a blank pad of paper. I never wrote more than a sentence or two; there was no content to my dreams of being a writer, just the romance of writing. I also took to carrying around a pen and pad and making notes about events, people, conversations—gathering the makings of future writings.

The same adventures that beckoned to Stephen beckoned to me. I read *Portrait of the Artist as a Young Man* as I was preparing to leave my community for college and begin my landlocked voyage away from home. I decided that I needed to get away from home and encounter a larger world. I applied to Harvard College and got in. I knew nothing of life there or of the social demands it made on students, nor was I prepared for them. Still, leaving home and the Bronx was the adventure I wanted at that time in my life.

Living within a ghetto on the terms set up for it by the outside world is an insulating and isolating experience. It is not the same as creating your own community out of choice or love. A ghetto is separated. The culture of the ghetto is a response, both positive and negative, to the condition of being separated out. In the case of my community the separating force was anti-Semitism, just as racism is a similar force in the lives of many of my students. That doesn't mean that the culture of the ghetto is all simply a response to the forces of exclusion and rejection. On the contrary, it is full of celebrations, ingenuity, tricks, advice, and encouragement. It is a source of self-respect and dignity, though not unmixed with hints of shame and stigmatization. It teaches lessons of resistance and survival. I remember, for example, a joke my grandfather told me which has stuck in my head and become a talisman for me. It was a source of strength when I encountered anti-Semitism, as I did in my undergraduate years at Harvard. The story is about an underwear manufacturer, Mr. Goldstein, and J. P. Morgan. It seems that Goldstein was the major manufacturer of men's underwear and handkerchiefs in the world, and therefore was as rich as J. P. Morgan. In fact, he bought a house right next door to Morgan and furnished it, down to the tea spoons and napkins, exactly like Morgan furnished his house. One Sunday, Morgan got up early and went out to mow his lawn. Goldstein also got up early and went out to mow his lawn with the identical gold-plated mower that Morgan used. They mowed up and down the rows of their lawns until they both ended up at a wall that divided their property. Goldstein looked over at Morgan, said hello, and told Morgan that he thought Morgan had a beautiful house, a house so beautiful that he bought one just like it. Morgan grumped and spit out an acknowledgment that Goldstein had indeed created a copy of his house. Then Goldstein continued, "But Morgan, there's just one thing I have to tell you. My house is more valuable than yours." This was too much for the giant of banking, who turned nasty and demanded that Goldstein explain to him how it was possible for Goldstein's house to be worth more than Morgan's house. "Well," replied Goldstein, "I don't live next door to a Jew."

I remember asking my grandfather what that joke meant, and he said, "Once a Jew, always a Jew—but we can do anything they can do and be better at it." This wild flight of the imagination was both a condensation of the history of anti-Semitism and advice about being strong in spite of it.

Education is intimately tied to the nature of the situation in which it takes place and the moral values of the teacher, students, and community. This implies understanding, to the degree possible, the cultural, social, political, class, and economic circumstances of students, teachers, and the community. It also means taking account of the historical moment in which one is teaching. There is no single best way to go about teaching. In the midst of the Civil Rights Movement it was important to center learning on participation and social action. During the Reagan and Bush years it became necessary to center on resistance, social conscience, and the development of an awareness of social struggles throughout the world. Now combating hopelessness is our major challenge.

Thus, before designing a strategy for teaching and learning, it's essential to analyze the situation and learn about the community. It is also crucial to research a variety of strategies, skills, techniques, and materials in order to be able to discover what has the greatest chance of working while at the same time maintaining students' dignity and self-respect in a particular context. The curriculum should emerge from this analysis. No two classes, even though they may cover the same subject with youngsters of the same age, should be structured in the same way. Their common needs, such as certain analytic skills and problem-solving techniques, must be addressed and they must encounter and master complex texts and relevant information. In addition, the moral values implicit in democratic ideas must be lived as well as taught in all educational contexts. But beyond that, educational planning must be situational.

One example comes to mind. During the 1970s I worked with the Center for Open Learning and Teaching in Berkeley, California, helping teachers and community groups plan their own schools. In one instance we were asked to help a farm workers' cooperative plan and build a nursery school for their own children. The members of the co-op were Mexican-American and Filipino and lived in California's Central Valley. Though they were poor, they had many skills, knew how to work cooperatively, and made the most of scarce resources. With the help of some community members and a community organizer, we spent time getting familiar with the situation before planning our work. We quickly discovered that members of the community had power tools and knew how to build furniture. A few people knew how to make posters and use a printing press. Many of the women owned sewing machines. There were a few fully bilingual people who could read and write in both English and Spanish. In other words, we discovered that the cooperative had all of the skills and tools needed to build and staff their own nursery school. Our job as educators was to help the people understand how they could use what they already had in a new way that would enable them to create their own school. They could create not merely the furniture and curtains, but the books, posters, and curriculum. They could teach their own children within the community and mold the school to fit the needs of their work and the values of their cultures.

Our intent was to concentrate the workshop on educational materials that could be made by the community with its own resources rather than bought. The workshop began, and we were the experts, supposed to make the presentation. However, what we showed and talked about came from our knowledge of the situation, and by the time the day was over, people had brought their tools and sewing machines. By the end of the workshop they had created blocks, a puppet theater and puppets, alphabet books, cutout letters and numbers, and math and language learning games—enough material to stock a small preschool. In addition, they learned how to use the materials and, from my perspective, were ready to develop a school of their own.

Education works best when it is grounded, when it merges the skills and knowledge of the community with the skills and knowledge of the educators. Often what we can do best as educators is show how resources, skills, knowledge, and culture can be brought to bear to enrich the lives of children. I have been criticized for my emphasis on the active role of a teacher, particularly by people who are sensitive to the damage bad teaching can do and have come to suspect all direct teaching. I agree that racism, sexism, impatience, the desire to track, stigmatize, mold, or control children's lives are negative forces. They damage children and are capable of setting up conditions of lifelong resentment, rage, and self-hatred. But there are teachers within the public schools across the country that do the opposite. They provide their students compassion and work from their pupils' strengths. They also love learning and have a passion to share what they know and are learning with their students.

And I love teaching. For me, writing on a chalkboard and going on about something I am dying to share with my students is one of the greatest pleasures of teaching. I don't feel a need to force them to love what I love or learn what I have learned. I just want to have an occasion to inspire them. After all, I didn't invent Mozart, build Carnegie Hall, or know what my uncle Julius taught me before he took the initiative to teach me. Taking the initiative to teach well and with love has always been as important to me as providing my students with an opportunity to learn on their own.

There is a narrow but distinct line one has to walk between teaching content and skills that are expected of educated adults in our society and letting students follow their inner needs and explore those areas of learning where they have particular skills or affinities. There are times when an opening occurs for a child, when some art, craft, skill, or technology speaks directly to something within her or him, when mathematics or chemistry or poetry seem magical. At those times it is essential to help the child follow that inner desire and let other things slide for a while. Of course, not every child will manifest such a center, and a general flow of creative learning must continue in the class. But there is no need for everyone to be learning the same things at all times. Teaching well means encouraging the widest diversity and greatest depth of learning possible, and always being open to adding a new dimension or theme to what one is doing in order to tease the genius out of one more child. It consists, among all of its other roles, in providing students with opportunities to have encounters with learning that might transform their lives.

This means freeing youngsters from the traps of a set curriculum, letting them on occasion wander aimlessly across subject matter, craft, art, technology. It consists of supporting them when they try things they never imagined they could do, and often of setting up those things. It means creating opportunities, setting challenges, providing resources, and most of all suggesting that students listen to inner voices, that they embrace their own Masked Riders, that they take sea voyages like Tod Moran's, that they feel free to reject what other people want them to learn and not learn anything that invades their personal space in a way that erodes their confidence, dignity, and self-respect. Education requires helping students develop the strength to resist and at the same time grow comfortable with their inner voices and listen carefully to the advice and confidences of people they love or respect. It means helping them learn how to find teachers, ask for help, and experience the exhilaration of learning unfettered by grades, critiques, exhibitions, and other forms of display. It is the opposite of training students to fit into a social niche, a job in someone else's corporation, a role in someone else's hierarchy. On the contrary, it consists of helping young people learn how to create a niche, find a vocation, and live democratically.

Teaching is a form of questing with my students for their inner strengths. It is a matter of patience and faith—the patience to let affinities, skills, talents, and dreams emerge; the faith that within everyone, no matter how damaged, hostile, or withdrawn, there is some unique constellation of abilities, sensitivities, and aspirations that can be discovered, uncovered, or rescued. The concept of failure has to be eliminated from the mind of the teacher. Therefore, teaching has to be considered an absurd activity, a joyful foolishness. No evidence of the senses, no social, political, or economic condition, no current state is adequate to cause one to abandon hope for what a young person might become.

Teaching is a romantic calling—this in the face of all of the horrors we see and experience every day, of the misery and hopelessness inflicted on children, of societal put-downs of romanticism in the name of "the real world," of the difficulty of the task of helping all of the children we take responsibility for. When hope fades in a teacher's heart, it becomes impossible to draw out a young person for her or his own sake and for the contribution their specialness can make to the whole of society.

"But what about preparing children for the demands of the *real world*?" I hear that echoing every time I use the word "romantic" or talk about hope or love instead of the curriculum. I'm not too sure I know about the real world. Certainly, young people need to learn how to read intelligently, write coherently, and be able to understand how numbers function in their lives and do calculations. They should also know about their own culture and have a grasp of how the economy and society work. They certainly should know the Bill of Rights. There are many things that people should know and can learn over the course of thirteen years of primary and secondary schooling. However, the specifics of how, when, and in what context they learn these things are subject to debate. Even more, the need to fill up all of one's learning time with the specific aim of adjusting to corporate or governmental ideas of who one should be and what vocation one should be channeled into is dysfunctional for individuals and unfair to the majority of people in our society. This is particularly true in a society that does not guarantee students jobs for which their education has prepared them.

The freedom to make a life for oneself based on fulfilling work that one freely chooses is, for me, an essential aspect of life in a democracy, and if so-called real-world education denies this freedom, then it must be opposed as dangerous for children. That doesn't imply that we become "unreal" and deceive our students about the obstacles to fulfillment and the need for intelligent navigation and thoughtful compromise. Rather, it means that we help them keep their dreams while struggling to survive in practical ways. It means we keep our teaching focused on hope and possibility rather than on conformity and mere survival.

Education that channels children also sorts out those children who do not fit in. These children become dispensable—a burden—and are stigmatized and labeled. From another, more democratic point of view they are the victims of a society that elevates competition to an absolute value. As Thurgood Marshall said in reference to racial segregation, "Stigmatic injury is real, it's cruel, and it's forbidden by the Constitution."*

Over the past few years I have been working with youngsters who, by the age of seven, have been burdened with almost as many categories of stigmatization and labels as they have years. The roll call reads: attention deficit disorder, at risk, fetal alcohol syndrome, learning-disabled, culturally disadvantaged, dysfunctional family, underachiever, and so on. When I meet the children, it would be easy to interpret their lack of confidence and defiant attitudes as confirmations of the labels that imprison them. Take William, for example. One of his aunts asked me to help him with his school work. He was seven and had already been tested and classified as a problem learner. It would have been easy to confirm the school's diagnosis. William didn't know the alphabet, or at least when I asked him to identify letters, he

---

*Quoted in Carl T. Rowan, *Dream Makers, Dream Breakers: The World of Justice Thurgood Marshall* (Boston: Little, Brown, 1993), p. 10.

called each one "an abc." He told me that nickels, pennies, and dimes were coins and insisted that the shiny new penny was worth more than an old dime. He couldn't or wouldn't count up to ten. He didn't look straight at me, and when we shook hands, his hand went limp. I asked him a few questions, and he mumbled some incomprehensible sounds while his aunt informed me that he was in speech therapy and had a hard time with language. It would have been easy to stay at the surface and accept that this child had limitations and then to limit my aspirations for him. But my experience has taught me that what I was seeing was the shell of a child, his protective covering, the behavior he adopted in order to conform to the expectations adults had created for him. He was sure he was a failure and that it was somehow his and his parents' fault. There was no one to take his part and protect him from the stigma system, and so he became part of it, a confirmation and justification of it.

I figured the best way to approach William was to neglect his shell and assume that he knew a lot more than he was letting on. So I took out a few shiny pennies and told him I'd be delighted to exchange the pennies for his dirty dimes. He smiled slyly and turned his face away so I couldn't catch the smile. I caught him out. He knew perfectly well what he could buy for a dime and what he could buy for a penny.

Then I asked him if he knew how to play baseball, and he looked at me tentatively. I opened a closet where I keep my baseball bats and gloves, a variety of balls, jump ropes, several bows and arrows, two styrofoam swords, three pairs of boxing gloves (two child-sized and one adult-sized), and a whole miscellany of other playthings I've accumulated over the years. I took out a bat, several gloves, and a soft baseball and asked William if he'd like to play catch with me. He shrugged his shoulders, put his head down again, and I got up and walked out with the bat, gloves, and ball. He followed.

I handed him a glove and his whole demeanor changed. He pounded his fist in the glove and assumed an infielder's stance. We played catch and then he took a turn hitting and hit the ball into the bushes. During our play we chatted about his favorite baseball teams and the players he admired. He mentioned an uncle who was playing pro ball and said that was his dream too. After we played around for a while, I told William's aunt that we had done enough for the day and that if William wanted to come back we could play again. And I added that William had shown me enough for me to know, as an experienced teacher, that he could read, write, and do anything academically he wanted to with time and support. I would help him. His problems were a crowded classroom and teachers who did not know how to help him. I put the matter as judiciously as I could, and his aunt understood.

There were no specific and documented reasons why William couldn't learn to read and do math if he wanted to, and I didn't care how long it took. There were risks—he might not ever choose to learn to read. William had friends in the same situation he was in, a future generation of school failures, who would become problems for themselves and the community. And there were the teachers at the school who were comfortable with the failure system and resisted efforts at change over the years. They had the power to undo anything I did if William and his aunt didn't prove strong enough.

Over the past few years I've seen William on a regular basis. Now he reads and also likes to read. He doesn't like school but knows he has to cope with it and does well, even though this aspect of his life pains me. I wish the school would change or start from scratch, but I won't mix up my efforts to change the school with William's present need to do well, even on the school's own pathetic terms.

What did I do to help William? Not much. We read a few

minutes a day for a while, discussed letters and sounds, played
baseball, counted coins, made a target and shot bows and arrows,
read some more, looked at pictures in books and talked about the
pictures. Sometimes I read a story, sometimes he made up one
after looking at the pictures. Rather than worry about teaching
him to read right away, I was teaching the first lesson he needed,
given his school history. That lesson could be called "I won't be
stupid" or "I won't let them make me stupid" or "I'm not stupid
no matter what they say." William began to master it informally by
opening himself up to learning and playing without worrying
about failing. He also learned it because we talked about it. I was
explicit in telling him that the school can often be wrong and that
he was smart. Children need to hear that from an adult; they need
to be told that this foolish system is not their fault, that all adults
do not honor it, that there are teachers both within and outside of
it that care about all children and believe that the way the system
works is wrong.

Stupidity is learned. I first encountered this idea about twenty-
five years ago and it has stuck in my mind like a melody—recur-
rent, persistent, and insidiously transforming. The anthropologist
Jules Henry said in his book *Culture Against Man*:

> Children everywhere have been trained to fit culture as it exists; and to
> the end that they should not fail to fit, man has used the great ingenu-
> ity of which he is capable. As a device for teaching what was necessary
> ...education became an instrument of...learning to be stupid.*

The idea that stupidity is learned, that people can reach the
point where they will do things that they know are foolish and
against their better interests, always echoes in my mind as I try to
understand how children come to hate themselves in school. As a
young teacher, I realized how I acted in complicity with the stu-

*(New York: Vintage, 1965), p. 320.

pidity system and forced my students into it at the same time. My students had to ask permission to go to the bathroom. Out of my own fear of loss of control, I tried to keep everything silent in the room; I asked my students to do worksheets that I thought were a waste of time, to read and regurgitate history texts that I knew told lies, and to walk down the hall in straight lines when we would all have been more comfortable chatting and strolling in informal groups.

As I learned how to be comfortable as a teacher, form a sane curriculum, and help my students participate in their own learning, it became clear that one of my central goals as a teacher was to resist stupidity at all costs and to help my students do it too.

In William's case, he had learned that he wasn't smart enough to read or do math like the other children. He accepted that judgment and the judgment that there was something wrong with his head (attention deficit disorder), his parents and his community (at-risk). All of this apparatus has in overt and covert ways trained him to accept the fact that in school he was and would be dumb. Even the remedial classes he was put in treated him like a hospital case and reinforced his feeling of inferiority. My first job was to help him unlearn his sense of failure. Then he had to develop mechanisms to protect himself against feeling inferior when confronted by standardized tests, his teacher's scrutiny, and the academically marginalized role that he played in his classroom. The best way for that to happen was for him to learn to read out of school and then apply those skills in school on his own terms and in his own way. So far, he has been remarkably successful at doing that, and consequently he has become free to discover what he wants to learn and to uncover some convergence between his strengths, his dreams, and the kinds of things people do in the world as they get older and become independent.

Not all youngsters have to go through such a tortuous route to reach themselves, but even some of the most motivated students can fall into the stigma system and its mechanisms of induced stupidity. One particular youngster (no longer a youngster, he must be around forty now) comes to mind. Lenny Pickett came to Other Ways, a high school I directed and taught at in Berkeley from 1968 to 1970, directly from Provo Park without taking the more usual route through a counselor or teacher at Berkeley High School. I don't remember our first meeting, but I do recall that he was about to be thrown out of Berkeley High School and was sought by truant officers for not attending school. This happened because he insisted upon practicing his saxophone all day and felt school kept him from what he really needed to do. He didn't want to take English, math, etc., and then, as the high school principal insisted, play music as an after-school activity. He didn't want to hang around in study hall or have one-to-one tutoring in special-education classes. He drove the authorities crazy because he had never learned to take their threats to fail him or stigmatize him seriously. He had not learned to listen to them and therefore was a bad example, a troublemaker who was driven out of the school and into the park—where in fact he practiced his saxophone. If he had been rich instead of poor, he might have been provided with private tutors and would have had no problems with any educational authorities.

During Lenny's first few days at Other Ways, he got to sample all of our classes, which were designed, often with the help of our students, to deal with relevant and current issues, to open up new areas of learning, and to provide skills in the arts, literature, and the sciences. We tried to shape our curriculum to the needs and interests of our students. Still, up to the time of Lenny, we insisted that anyone who wanted to be part of the school had to participate in a minimum number of classes in English, math, and social studies. We had a choice of many classes in each area and somehow we managed to keep everyone interested or at least present.

Lenny was different. He told me he didn't want groovy math, groovy English, groovy social studies. He wanted to play his sax, and if Other Ways wouldn't let him, he'd go back to the park.

I had to face the fact that though Other Ways was a different school, a very personalized one with many choices for the students and a great deal of student control, Lenny slipped outside of even our difference. It surprised me, but I became anxious that if an exception was made for Lenny all of the students would demand to do as they pleased. I thought I was beyond worrying more about the rules than the lives of the students, but I wasn't. It was a struggle to break our own rules, but since no other school showed the slightest inclination to welcome him, I did and he became a student at Other Ways. He never took an English, math, social studies, or any other class. But he did join the community of the school and provided the musical accompaniment to our guerrilla theater. We worked it out so that Lenny could get piano lessons, learn to read and write music, and practice as long and as well as he could. He knew how to find saxophone teachers on his own. We also worked it out that he would compose and perform his own songs and give us a tape for graduation credit.

During his time at Other Ways, Lenny played in a number of bands, participated in street theater, went with the guerrilla theater troupe to New Mexico to appear in the film *Billy Jack*, practiced a lot, and was a delightful spirited presence at school. None of the other students ever objected. In fact, they were proud to have him among us.

I don't remember whether Lenny formally graduated but do recollect that as soon as he turned eighteen he joined the band Tower of Power and now, at about forty, is still composing and playing his saxophone with the Saturday Night Live Band and the Borneo Horns.

Most of us are not as focused or obsessed as Lenny was as a youngster. However, I have never known a child, no matter how superficially unmotivated she or he might seem, whose indifference, hopelessness, or rage did not mask a lively imagination and dreams of challenging work, lasting love, and a fullness of being. I believe the same thing is also true of adults. Some people are bold enough to do what they want to do despite social and economic pressures. Others are lucky enough to have their dreams and aspirations coincide with financial rewards and social status. Other people channel their dreams into hobbies that range from collecting stamps or beer cans to painting, building models, broadcasting on shortwave radio, managing Little League teams, etc. There are even people who abandon fairly successful careers, downscale their lives, and take the risk of doing what they love instead of working at jobs that diminish them as people. However, many people's lives have been determined by economic necessity and social oppression, and their dreams have been put aside. The momentum of their lives and the hardships imposed upon them by our society, which is so deficient in compassion, cause them to give up on themselves. Dreams and high expectations become a burden, a constant source of guilt and shame.

Along with poverty, abuse, endemic violence, or neglect, schooling can cause the abandonment of hope and the development of apathy. In too many high schools young people are channeled into a few specific vocations by counselors who make judgments using a narrow range of measurements of school performance to determine what they think is appropriate for particular students' future lives. They are often guided by cultural stereotypes. In addition, they value certain occupations and denigrate others. For example, students who do well in school are usually discouraged from going into film, theater, art, music, journalism, photography, furniture making, comic-book and other forms of illustration, weaving, cooking—any number of occupations that do not fit the narrow range of corporate, professional, or academic careers. If a "good" student aspires to one of these nonsanctioned vocations, he is considered a failure and usually told he is selling himself short.

Many other students are not expected to succeed at all and are channeled to work in the woods dragging logs, to do rough construction, or to settle down and have children. Even when they have aspirations that are clear to themselves and their families, they are discouraged from following them. One student who works for me and is a Pomo Indian, for example, is a very gifted computer programmer and mathematician. His skills are either ignored at school or not even known. He has been channeled to junior college and is convinced that he does not have the skills or ability to go to a four-year college. This is directly against the clear evidence he shows during his work, which involves mathematics and complex computer programming. I have to overcome his internalization of the school's judgment of his strengths and convince him to reach out, and it isn't easy. He is a victim of the suppression of his dreams caused by the low expectations (and I believe racism) of his teachers and by their narrow view of the kinds of things people can sensibly do with their lives. It would make sense for every teacher in the United States to read the U.S. Department of Labor's guide to professions and occupations and get a larger view of what people actually do with their lives, and let their students know about it. The more one knows what one might do, the easier it is to think through what one really cares to do, and the less chance there is that one might be caught up in alienating and, for many students, low-paying work.

Unfortunately, many students become accustomed to being treated as objects by people who control their access to higher learning, and too often these young people just give up on their aspirations. The role educators who care about the dreams of their students have to play involves figuring out how to get through the masks young people develop when they are under siege by the adult world. Sometimes the problem is schooling for stupidity. However, we have to remember that the schools are not the only forces that put many young people under siege. Poverty, abuse, endemic violence, or neglect also lead to indifference to learning. However, as teachers we cannot let the unfortunate circumstances of some of our students' lives undermine our efforts to reach through to the strong part of even the most hurting and damaged child.

"Failure" has a prominent place in the vocabulary of educational experts, although I don't believe it is a useful educational category. It does not help one teach, and it inhibits and suppresses learning. For example, children who cannot read at levels they are expected to simply cannot do certain things. Calling them failures tags an insult onto a statement of fact. We stigmatize their current inability by articulating it into a norming system when we should be going about inventing new ways to help students instead. Using the concepts of "failure" and "lack of motivation" becomes a substitute for the hard work of inventive teaching.

Recently, I have been teaching a class to other teachers about strategies for eliminating the concept of failure from the classroom without abandoning high standards. One of the sessions is devoted to teachers reflecting on their own schooling, and it's been astonishing how many people volunteer that they consider themselves, as adults, to be either A, B, C, D, or F people. Occasionally, that internalized identity comes out in discussion when someone doesn't follow an argument or feels they've missed a reference. The teachers say things like: "I didn't understand what you meant, but I'm just a C person," or "I'm an A and should understand, but I don't, maybe its my age," or "I'll never understand something that complex, I've been a D all my life."

Here's where the Masked Rider, my uncle Julius, Tod Moran, and Mozart come back into the story. As teachers, and I believe as parents and citizens too, we must return to the sources of our powers and joys no matter how difficult things seem in the present. We must refuse to perceive anyone, including ourselves, as failures. Teachers in particular have an obligation to work to sustain hope and to resist giving up on young people. One way to do this is to remember why one decided to teach in the first place. What images and metaphors come to mind when teachers think about the original inspiration they felt and their desires to spend their lives working with young people?

Teachers I know and work or teach with all have a bit of the dreamer and a bit of the missionary in them. They feel—or felt at one time in their lives—that their work among the young is not a matter of gaining power over students so much as providing them with power. One of the common reasons for becoming a teacher is to pursue a power-giving vocation. The specific reason might be to give children what you didn't get, or to give them what you got from special adults and see lacking in their lives. Rescue is another motive—the idea that education has a redemptive power to overcome the miseries of poverty or the injuries of class and race. Smaller insults to dignity and self-respect can also motivate a life of teaching—the idea that you can help people overcome the wounds inflicted by a cold culture on people who are considered too fat or thin, not pretty or handsome enough, from the "wrong" families or with the "wrong" attitudes. Implicit in the idea of the redemptive value of education is the notion that knowledge, art, craft, sensitivity, and the skills of reading, writing, and arithmetic are sources of personal as well as communal power. And implicit in the will to teach is the idea that teachers are transformers, that they can help people transform their lives in decent ways and in that manner contribute to the transformation of society. As I said before, teaching is essentially romantic—it is predicated on the idea that the world can get better than it is by the efforts of people, rather than by the movement of supraindividual processes.

The Masked Rider enticed me into willing encounters with the strange, the new, the unexplored territories beyond the Bronx that I didn't even know existed. Uncle Julius gave me maps of some of those territories and never asked anything back for himself but the pleasure of seeing me learn. Tod Moran tried to rescue his older brother, took on the task every young person has to confront of being stronger than the adults around them. The music of Mozart provided me with the kind of joy that hard times and hopelessness do not extinguish. I have taken from these encounters, and others I haven't written about, the metaphors that drive my teaching, just as I have taken from my grandparents and their world the central values of equity and justice that underpin my work. These metaphors and values provide me with tools of resistance when the inertia of systems and the rhetoric of success and failure, the insinuations of racism and class bias, and the enticement of blaming others for our collective failure to realize democratic visions tempt me or erode confidence in my own work and struggles.

Unfortunately, many teachers become socialized to taking power away from students, to judging, stigmatizing, and failing young people. These modes of thinking and functioning are learned in teacher-education schools, from colleagues and supervisors. They become habitual in schools predicated on the success of a few and the failure or marginalization of the majority. But they can be unlearned through a return to the original sources of one's love of learning and of teaching. We have to maintain faith in our students no matter how they might be performing in the present and find sources of that faith in ourselves and our friends, and in the tradition of those people who have struggled over the years to create decent schools.

We also have to understand ourselves as victims of the same system we are imposing on our students. That means accepting responsibility for the double task of protecting students from being defined in terms of external criteria and examining how that sorting system has affected our feelings. Learning along with one's students is one way to discover all of the hidden, suppressed, and forgotten strengths and dreams we teachers have. It is one of the gifts of teaching in a congenial setting where there is a sense of a common struggle to know more about the world and oneself.

About ten years ago I worked with a youngster who had a hard time talking and made no progress whatever with learning to read. The school tried to turn him into a stigma case, but his parents and I confronted the school at every point they tried to label him retarded or disturbed. I continued to work with him over the years, and though I tried every single technique and trick in my repertory, nothing worked. Last year, at the age of sixteen, Lawrence learned how to read. No one knows how. I certainly don't. At the beginning of his sophomore year in high school, he went to the school counselor and said he wanted to take the regular English class rather than the general remedial class he was scheduled to take. The counselor was hesitant and challenged him to read from the English textbook. He did, with ease, and passed freshman English that year. Now in his junior year, he is doing well in sophomore English and is determined to catch up with the rest of his class by the beginning of his senior year.

I asked Lawrence what happened, and he said he decided it was time and so he worked at it. He didn't know exactly how it happened, but after spending a summer fighting his way through several books, he found himself reading most things with ease. Fortunately, he was not trapped in the stigma system and did not have to prove himself in order to get out. Though he didn't have good grades, he was still a regular student on the margin of failure who showed sudden improvement. I like the mystery of it. Lawrence's parents and I are proud of the way we protected him and believed in him, and even prouder of the way in which he took control of his own learning.

The social use of the concept of motivation is analogous to that of the social use of the concept of failure. Students who don't respond in school and are not defiant are called unmotivated. They are treated as if they are in some way deficient. Sometimes this lack of motivation is attributed to their home or community or economic status. Sometimes it is blamed on the food they eat, the electric waves in their brains, or their parents' cultural background. All of this places the locus of motivation in the child. Lenny Pickett on this analysis was an unmotivated student since he refused to become involved in English or social studies.

The role of a teacher in this view of motivation is either to negate something about the child or her or his world, to repair something in the child, or, if the mode is benign, to seduce the child into doing things she or he doesn't care to do. If you drop the concept of motivation, though, and take a fresh look at a child who is refusing to do what you want, the situation changes. You then become an explorer with the goal of uncovering or helping your students uncover the gifts and strengths that can nurture them as they grow.

It is one thing to search with one student for those aspects of human activity attractive enough to engage her or his energy and intelligence. It is quite another to try to do this with a whole class. While I can spend time with William searching for the key to his connection with learning, I am hard-pressed to keep this questing on the agenda five hours a day, five days a week, with thirty children, many of whom reject anything I may present to them. Yet a considerable part of the craft of teaching well is learning to attend to the needs of many children while going about your business of teaching particular content. It takes skill and experience to maintain a personal relationship with each child while having to orchestrate a group and adhere to an instructional curriculum you may despise. I had a teacher in the fifth grade who pulled it off. Her name was Mrs. Katz, and our class was held in the boiler room of the school. It was just after World War II, and our school still had its victory garden where the students in the school grew vegetables to help the war effort. There must have been close to forty of us in the class. I loved big classes because it was easy to hide in them.

Hiding was one of my specialties in the fifth grade. I felt fat and ugly, and in addition to my asthma I had developed the habit of scratching my wrists to the point where they bled. I remember my wrists wrapped in gauze, both to facilitate healing and to prevent me from scratching. In class I sat toward the rear of the room, and during recital and question time kept my face hidden behind the book and never raised my hand. Most of the time I had fantasies about stepping into the pictures in the text and daydreamed an adventure. Since I was in a class of eager and bright students, there were always hand wavers to distract the teacher's attention. I now realize Mrs. Katz knew I was hiding and let me hide most of the time. She could have rooted me out, humiliated me in front of the class, or, worse, called in my parents and told them that I was an unmotivated student and that they had better get on with the job of motivating me.

My father had motivated me in the first grade when I simply ignored all of Mrs. Cooper's efforts to teach me reading. We were using the look-and-see method of reading and a Dick and Jane basal reader. Somehow learning to recognize the words "Dick," "Jane," and "Spot" didn't interest me. I liked my aunt Addie to read nursery rhymes and stories to me, enjoyed looking at picture books and making up stories, but this Spot thing made no sense to me whatever. Mrs. Cooper sent a letter home saying she wanted to have a conference with my father. In my working-class community, when you ask a father to come to school, you are asking him to give up a half day's work and therefore punishing the whole family. Something must be seriously wrong.

My father came, and Mrs. Cooper sat me down and asked me to read from the basal. I said "Spot" for "Dick," "Jane" for "Spot," and "Dick" for "run."

My father was more embarrassed than angry. How could a son of his who showed no obvious signs of stupidity not get it. And I didn't get it; it was all a game to me.

When we got home, I got it. My father said in no uncertain terms that I had to learn to read for the sake of my future, the family's pride, and the dignity of our community. It was my job. The next day he brought home a set of Dick and Jane readers he had bought downtown at Barnes and Noble. He gave me the books plus that day's copy of the *New York Times*. My job was to learn to read. Also, I had to cut out each occurrence of the word "the" in the headlines of the first few pages of the *Times* and paste it on a piece of paper. When I learned the word "the," he gave me another word to work on.

Behind all this was the not-so-subtle threat that something bad would happen to me if I didn't do what Mrs. Cooper wanted me to do—quick. I became motivated and learned how to do school reading in a few weeks at the most. It wasn't reading to me, not reading words that meant anything. It was doing my job, which, several years later, I was still doing fairly well and with equal lack of interest in Mrs. Katz's class.

Mrs. Katz never tried to motivate me. She let me hang in the middle of the class and daydream. I wasn't much of a trouble-maker then. Junior high was when I grew about six inches, became slim, and stretched out in defiance. But Mrs. Katz didn't let me get lost either. During yard time or just as we were returning from lunch, she hung out with her class and chatted with students individually or in small groups. There was nothing formal about it, nothing threatening. She was getting to know us, and I enjoyed those moments out of class with her.

One time she came up to me. I remember it was just in front of the irises we planted on the border of the victory garden. She asked me what I was thinking about when we did social studies and I hid behind my book. She asked the question in such a casual and uncritical way that I answered, "Pretending I'm in the pictures on the page."

Mrs. Katz responded that she thought it was wonderful that I had such a rich imagination and that some day I might like to draw my adventures or write about them or turn them into music. That was it. We went back to class and all semester she let me hide, though I always felt she and I were in complicity and getting away with something wonderful together. I even tried to please her in small ways like volunteering to do errands or wash the chalk-board after school.

That one moment when she revealed that she saw something in me worth honoring and respecting was the highlight of my elementary school career. Times like that are beyond motivation and go straight to the heart of helping people find out about their own internal necessities, of setting them on the road to discovering the person they must become if they are to live full and rich lives. They are moments when, as a teacher, the only thing you care about in someone else is what makes them strong, times when you see what someone could become if the world were a kinder and more welcoming place. And for students they are occasions for rejoicing in being themselves and no one else.

My own teaching is shaped by my dreams as a child and my school experience. I can connect with my students through myself as a child. It is important for teachers to connect their work with children with their own childhood aspirations and dreams as well as with their best and worst learning experiences. Reflecting on your own experiences with learning, both in school and outside of it, is a good way to begin to develop a philosophy of teaching and learning. The negative experiences are as valuable as the positive ones. And the unrequited longings of childhood are as useful in designing a program for young people as are actual achievements. Teaching, to come from the heart, must connect with the teacher's inner life and learning adventures. It is from that stance that one can develop judgment and sort through all of the programs and theories that "experts" throw at teachers.

In addition to reflection on one's own experiences, continual informal contact with students that allows them to reveal themselves and show their strengths and aspirations enhances the ability to teach well and reach students in ways that nurture them. This means talking with students about everything and nothing, responding in a personal way to their writing, asking them what they enjoy doing outside of the context of schoolwork. It implies listening very carefully to what they say and responding to their concerns and questions.

Being friendly to students can mean simple things like saying hello to them in the hall or on the streets, gestures that are not common in most schools, and can even get young teachers in trouble. This may sound silly to people who have never taught in public schools, but I remember in my early years getting bad evaluations for "socializing excessively with students." This criticism applied specifically, according to my principal, to the fact that I occasionally sat and chatted with my students in the lunchroom on my own time, and that I said hello to them in the halls and outside of the school. He told me that, in doing those things, I was not adequately professional and that my students wouldn't respect me. He certainly was professional in that sense, though there were no signs that the students respected him for his coldness. And I've always been more concerned with my work as a teacher and my relationships with my students than with the nature of my evaluations (though there have been times when I've made compromises to survive and continue to fight rather than be fired).

Undoubtedly, personalizing one's teaching means spending more time with students than most teachers are accustomed to doing. But schools have to have a feeling of family and teachers have to be approachable if students are to open themselves up and let their aspirations be heard and their hidden strengths discovered.

These informal moments should also be supplemented by serendipitous observations of individual children or groups of children made while carrying on work with the class. Teaching, in one of its many facets, means having antennae—ears and eyes—all over your body that pick up unspoken messages from students. Some of these extra organs are used to detect the imminence of trouble. Others seek out students' inner motivations or personal feelings. These all help create a comfortable and secure environment for learning. Another, less common use is to scan constantly for indications, not of defiance or internal motivation, but of potential sources of joy and pride. Sometimes a child who is usually quiet and bored will light up at a particular story or event. Or she or he might grab you at lunch and tell you about something that was exciting at home or on TV. Or a student who is always lively and overly enthusiastic becomes quiet and contemplative when a certain subject is introduced.

All of these might be indicators of some deep-seated, as yet unarticulated gift or desire to engage the world. Schools that teach only one thing or project only one or two models of how to live a rich and effective life marginalize many students' gifts and skills. With so many useful things people can do, it is pathetic for schools to focus on a few professions and careers. What untapped brilliance has remained dormant because young people didn't know what they might become? Potential is a mystery that must be actualized to be appreciated. That's why I attribute all unknown potentials to every child and try to provide every opportunity I can dream up for children to try out different ways of being in the world.

It is not enough just to perceive what students might be or aspire toward. One has to follow up and give students gifts that take them into their dreams. A chess set, a simple electronics kit, an introduction to someone who does the kind of work a student indicates he or she might like to try, a trip to a laboratory or back-stage at a theater, a book that seems like it might speak to a child the way *The Tattooed Man* spoke to me—all are gifts that might change children's lives, create hope and joy where there was emptiness. Gift giving is essential to teaching. And gifts are always returned—not to the teacher but to the whole class, for they set up a spirit of mutual concern. When a teacher indicates a personal interest in each child and feeds children with fruitful learning, students begin to take greater interest in each other. And they can come to feel what we adults should but often don't feel—that young people are welcome in the world, and are a pleasure to be with and to know.

In schools these days there is a tendency to try to protect students from the horrors of life, and this results in casting a negative pall over the whole process of education. Over the past three years I have visited schools throughout the United States and have worked with educators who are trying to create decent places of learning in the midst of social chaos and economic despair. What I see in these and other schools is overriding frustration with a world defining itself through prohibitions and a presentiment of imminent explosions and storms.

You can often tell a lot about a school by what is displayed in the halls and on classroom walls. Here is what one usually sees these days in high schools:

AIDS-prevention information
antidrug and -alcohol posters and pamphlets
antirape and date-rape material
antihomophobic, antiracist, and antisexist material
graphics produced by safe-sex and abstinence programs
antiviolence and sometimes antigun documents

*discipline and search codes

*testimonies of people (often students) about how they resisted or kicked dysfunctional habits

*statements about the importance of individual effort and the virtues of competition and free enterprise

It is much rarer to see affirmations of cultural or communal pride, artistic integrity, and the pleasures and joys of being alive. Joy seems to have absented itself from the schools. It is time to get tough, the politicians say, and the schools echo: Time to get down to hard work, decreased expectations, and a sacrifice of one's self to some amorphous and clichéd desire to have the United States dominate the world.

This negativity is conveyed to students whose lives are defined by the violence they live or witness via the media. It is a major impediment to learning that confronts caring teachers who want their students to live full and flourishing adult lives. Teaching in the absence of hope is a burden that can demoralize even the most caring and energetic person, and yet it afflicts the lives of most sensitive teachers these days. It is up to us to negate this negativity—not through a denial of the horrible things that do exist but through the affirmation of possibility and the energy and love we can bring to our students. We have to be hopeful despite the obvious despair in the lives of our children and communities and society. We have to be dreamers ourselves and not allow foolish accusations about being out of touch with the real world to bother us. What is real is less important than what can be made real through our efforts and our students' untapped brilliance and boundless energy.

It's funny how unexpected brilliance can be brought forth through caring education. There is no guarantee that every student will find some life-centering vocation or love in work. But the freedom to seek a decent place for oneself in the world and the ability to experiment with possibilities without being forced into other people's agendas or used to produce profit for others are central to achieving a full personal life. I believe that encouraging students' quests for their place and their gift and their role in the larger society must be central to all of our teaching. *The Tattooed Man* is my symbol for such a quest—my discovery of the book and the sea voyage it describes. It made my world larger, provided me with a romantic vision of what I might become and pointed me toward writing and serving, with joy, on the tramp steamer and not the luxury liner. I now understand that though the voyage of the tramp steamer *Araby* took me away from the world I grew up in, it also kept me there. The symbol of the humble and dangerous voyage on a rotting ship in perilous seas is much more compelling to me that of flying across the ocean on the SST. I prefer being in the water to speeding over it.

The Tattooed Man ends with the *Araby* arriving home:

> As he turned and looked across the straining hawsers at the *Araby*, lying there so quietly, so lifeless, yet withal so gallant, he [Tod Moran] felt his heart tug at its moorings. Here, this wouldn't do! At this rate, within a month, he'd want to be at sea again. He stood there in silence, while about him the life of the water front flowed on.*

Tod Moran's voyage and what I learned from it has stayed with me for over forty years, as has the Masked Rider. I am incurably romantic and refuse to be discouraged by the so-called real world. I still have asthma, though it is usually under control. Every once in a while I get that clutch in my chest and feel the same anxiety at dusk that I did as a child. Fears and early terrors may recede, but they don't disappear. They just become smaller

---

Tattooed Man, p. 331.

when your world gets bigger. I am lucky—I love to teach and love to write. In both of them I struggle against the misery and violence, the simple injustice of so many people's everyday lives.

There is also something of the romantic in all of the children I've taught, and in many of the teachers I know and work with. I try to nurture it. This romantic sensibility amounts to the sense that wonderful things can happen in the world, to anyone, no matter how terrible and hopeless things seem at present. This absurd hope and the joy the hope itself brings can lead to affirmation and experimentation, to taking a chance on oneself and saying "I must do this" and going where it takes you with all the resources you can muster no matter how meager. It is an affirmation of the inner strength that, for many children in our society, is under assault all the time. I know of no finer gifts we adults, teachers or not, can give to children than nonnegotiable love, support, and all of the resources we can muster as they learn what they must do and resist doing what is foreign and alien to their internal imperatives. A decent world can only be made by people whose growth has not been stunted by the imperatives of others.

Excellence, Equality, and Equity

In 1910 THE psychologist Edward Thorndike, a professor at Columbia Teachers College, collected over twenty thousand samples of handwriting by fifth- through eighth-graders. Together with a team of handwriting "experts," he identified what he felt to be ideals and standards for penmanship and then ranked the samples in order of "excellence" from one to ten. Thorndike's assumptions that it was possible to set up such standards of excellence and to make this ranking have changed children's lives irrevocably ever since. Once handwriting could be measured, handwriting textbooks could be created to conform to Thorndike's standards and schools could be required to teach to level ten rather than help each student develop a legible, fluid and personal style of writing.

I remember the torture of handwriting classes in elementary school, of writing with a standard pen and nib, having to be careful not to get ink all over my hands and shirt. I also remember being judged according to the standard of excellent handwriting set by my teachers. I never measured up to it even though I still believe my "level seven," "B—" handwriting is quite legible and reflects my character more than the narrow, slanted, more formal script of level ten.

In addition to Thorndike's work on handwriting, standards for English composition and arithmetic were also being developed between 1910 and 1920. Embodied in these early efforts was the idea that intelligence and academic achievement could somehow be related, and that every academic subject must have a unique hierarchical structure ranging in levels from bad to best. The idea that there might be many forms of excellence was not entertained by the original test makers.

Great impetus was given to the test-making and test-giving industry during World War I when the United States Army adopted a series of group tests to decide who was fit for service, who should be channeled to menial and grunt labor, and who should be sent to officers training school. From September 1917 to January 1919, the army tested 1,726,960 people and thus began the enormous growth of the educational-psychology business and the testing industry.

Of course, the army test makers and the test givers were educated, white, middle-class men who did not consider their perspective of power to be a biasing factor. The tests assumed that excellence in reading, writing, and other school-related skills was a good predictor of military leadership (though if I had to serve, I'd rather be under someone who had fifteen years' experience leading a construction gang than someone who had put in fifteen years on Chaucer). Not surprisingly, college-educated, upper-middle- and upper-class individuals performed best and were chosen as officers because of their presumed superiority in intelligence. Working-class and poor men were put in the infantry and sent to the front lines. Blacks were channeled to menial roles serving the whole white military establishment.

It may be that these class- and race-bound test results actually surprised the test makers. However, there is some evidence that bias was intentionally built into early tests. In a 1925 issue of *Crisis*, W. E. B. Du Bois mentions that a battery of achievement tests was given to blacks and whites in Louisville. The whites were embarrassed when the blacks did as well as they did. The tests were withdrawn and "renormed," a euphemism for "readjusted," so the results would come out "right."

The handwriting standards and the army exam are examples of norming excellence. And as these tests make perfectly clear, excellence is a matter of judgment. So rather than talk about what is excellent, what is standard, what conforms to rules and laws and tests and society, perhaps we should talk instead about equity. W. G. Secada was quoted in the *First Annual Yearbook of the Bank Street College of Education* as characterizing equity in the following way:

> The heart of equity lies in our ability to acknowledge that, even though our actions might be in accord with a set of rules, their results may be unjust. Equity goes beyond following the rules, even if we have agreed that they are intended to achieve justice. . . . Educational equity, therefore, should be construed as a check on the justice of specific actions that are carried out within the educational arena and the arrangements that result from those actions.

At the heart of commitment to equity is the sentiment that what is just and what is legal do not necessarily coincide, and that struggling for justice demands resisting or changing rules if they conflict with one's notion of justice. This implies appeal to moral rather than political or legal authority. Appeal to moral authority, however, does not involve statute, citation, or precedent. It is a matter of vision, commitment to ideas of good and evil, and decisions to act on the side of good.

Similarly, in determinations of excellence there exist personal and cultural commitments to a notion of what is best that go beyond objective formulation and certitude. Therefore, arguing for a particular stance on equity or a specific definition of excellence is as much a matter of rhetoric, storytelling, and anecdote as it is a question of marshaling evidence and producing chains of reasoning.

A number of years ago I visited an elementary school in southern Texas. In the hallway outside the principal's office was an elaborate, commercially manufactured display welcoming students, parents, and visitors to the school. The slogan of the display, GREAT THINGS HAPPEN TO CHILDREN LIKE OURS, was spelled out in letters three feet high. Under the letters were four larger-than-life cutout figures of children, all of whom were white like the principal. The children were beaming with pride; they all had new book bags and shiny lunch boxes. The principal pointed out the exhibit to me, of what he described as an expression of school spirit.

One hundred percent of the children in this economically depressed neighborhood school were Mexican or Mexican-American (Chicano). There was not one child who looked anything like the children on the walls. Most of the students in the school participated in the free-lunch program and never brought lunch boxes to school, because they had nothing to put in them.

When I suggested to the principal that this display might present a negative image to the students and community, I was told that I didn't understand. The children on the wall were models for his student body, examples of what they could achieve if only they tried. When I asked him what he imagined the students thought about seeing those models day after day and knowing that they didn't look like any children at the school, he launched into a tirade against multiculturalism, told me his goal was to make the school monolingual in English, and chattered away about the good old days when students tried to do their work and parents supported the administration. Now, he concluded, students couldn't learn and parents didn't care. He assured me that his staff had tried everything in their power to make the students learn but the students just weren't up to the rigors of education in the United States. When I asked him if all of the students were recent immigrants, as he had just implied, he stared at me blankly.

I dropped these issues with him but did spend time with the parents and teachers who had invited me to visit the school, many of whose families had lived in the community for generations. During our conversations the parents expressed extreme frustration. The teachers characterized the overall feeling about their students' school careers as one of depression. I wasn't sure what they meant by "depression" and asked them to explain the specific dynamics of their distress. The explanations that emerged during several days of conversation were directly tied to conflicts between their view of equity and the principal's notion of excellence.

To the principal, equality meant that every child had the same opportunity to read the same textbooks, take the same tests, answer the same questions in class, and thus to excel. The content of the tests, the nature of the test questions, and the skew of teacher expectations were ostensibly not factors that might interfere with or inhibit learning. An understanding of the cultural strengths of the parent community was not deemed relevant to the question of how students might best succeed in school.

For the parents and the two teachers these issues were central to their considerations of equity, which was more important to them than equality. They believed that the equal opportunity to read biased texts was not equitable. In fact, they knew it insulted and punished their children. They felt that the school was making their smart children ignorant. The word "their" was operative. The children were not just students thrown into a system of competition that would judge their competence and channel their futures. These children were the future, the hope of creating better lives while maintaining personal and cultural integrity. Very few of the parents had any intention of giving up allegiance to their Mexican origins or renouncing the Spanish language. They had relatives across the border and lived in two countries, spoke two languages, and lived within one cultural tradition while entering another. Multiculturalism was a matter of everyday existence for them and their children. The issue of equity was, specifically, how the reality of their existence would be honored by the school their children attended and reflected in the school's concept of excellence. It was a question of how respect for the children would pervade the way in which they were taught and the subjects they were taught.

The depression these teachers and parents talked about came about to a considerable degree because they knew the history of Mexico and Texas better than the school people and the textbooks. They had relatives who had made it or who had been victims of it. Textbook misrepresentations were not mere factual errors or omissions but direct and unambiguous insults. When, for example, the junior high school textbook they showed me claimed that "the first people to settle Texas came from New England and Virginia," the community and the children were insulted. When Spanish-speaking children who had come from decent schools in Mexico were given mathematical word problems in English and then judged deficient in math because they couldn't solve them, the situation was depressing.

In this community, children of Mexican origin were constantly put in positions in which they couldn't prove what they knew and were treated as intellectually deficient because of the cultural biases of the system. The depression was a covert acknowledgment of the lack of equity in their children's education. Equity would mean their children would be honored for the people they were and be welcomed to participate in a complex democracy that had high regard for them. The reality was that their children were being asked to give up pride and self-respect as the price of membership in an alleged democracy.

This is not unique to people of Mexican descent in Texas; African Americans, for example, still struggle for equity in our ostensibly multicultural society. If "equity," however, becomes a euphemism for "cultural conformity," we are no closer to true democratic citizenship than before.

If the repudiation of one's birthright becomes a prerequisite for the attainment of equality, and if equality means that everyone has an equal chance to admire the monocultural dreams of West Europeans, we are on the wrong track. If a school curriculum denigrates one's ancestors, religion, and contributions to the history of the human race, and denies one's full dignity—that is, if it teaches the superiority of one segment of a democratic society over others—it is damaging to the minds and spirits of all children: those taught that their cultures are secondary and those given the false security of believing they are the creators of culture. An equitable curriculum must affirm all people as creators of culture and honor the multiplicity of human efforts to come to terms with living on earth.

It may seem that I am overstating the degree to which the myths of West European culture are accepted as norms and imposed on children of other cultures. I want to cite a young people's geography book published by a subsidiary of Random House in 1992 called *Where on Earth: A Geografunny Guide to the Globe*, by Paul Rosenthal. On page 84 of the book there is a comic strip entitled "Europe." In the fifth panel Eastern Europe is referred to as "a jumble of cultures, languages and religions, whose borders are still changing," whereas, according to the author, "Western Europe's borders have been stable for the past two hundred years." One has to wonder how much geohistory the author used in his research. In 1793 there was no Italy, Germany, or Austria. There were a number of border changes in Western Europe after the First World War, during the Third Reich, and in the last few years. It's hard to imagine where the author came up with this oversimplification, though perhaps he too was a victim of the myth of a stable and culturally superior Western Europe. This guess is reinforced by the last panel, which shows a middle-class couple looking at a neatly planned garden with plots labeled Sweden, France, Spain, Portugal. The caption is "Europe, it is like a carefully tended garden." The man is saying, "Perhaps France could use some fertilizer," and the woman comments, "My, what a lovely Europe."

Tell that to the Catalonians, Walloons, Irish, Scots, Welsh, and northern Italians.

On page 38 there is a similar comic about South America, with captions such as "Home to many famous plants and animals"; "The Amazon—world's oldest jungle"; and "The fragile environment of the rain forest survives through cooperation." Only one human is pictured, a man wearing a sombrero and a serape who lives in the Patagonian desert and says, "Not so hot ...," to which a stone responds, "Sez you." This is in contrast to the nineteen people shown on the page devoted to Europe. No tended garden here.

The negative aspects of this kind of pseudohistory and geography presented as truth to children are damaging to everyone, including people of European-American descent. But specifically it leads to the kind of depression evident in that school in Texas, among those who are misrepresented.

This depression stems from the sense that the people in power are ignorant and biased and that you have no way to let them know it. It also comes from the fact that it isn't fair that members of some groups have to be less than themselves to be part of a so-called democratic society. Or that children can be punished simply for being who they were. In the context of schools, equity and multiculturalism are inextricable.

Multiculturalism is at the center of the struggle for fairness. Decency and depression are but first responses to inequity. Often they are followed by rage and then by organized dissent. The people I worked with in southern Texas got beyond their depression and as their first goal decided to persuade the current principal to leave. They chose two strategies. The first was to create a report card to evaluate the principal, a technique used earlier by the United Bronx Parents. The report card was designed to resemble the actual report card children received quarterly at the school, but it was bilingual. The categories to be graded ranged from "cooperates with parents," "has good working habits," "motivates student performance," "is effective in motivating staff to teach basic skills," "produces high test scores on a school-wide basis," to "creates a school environment that respects the community." These categories were developed in a series of workshops conducted by parents and some community organizers.

The workshops themselves were extremely valuable as exercises in community self-education. It was the first time that uninhibited public debates about the schools had occurred, a first step in the community's having a voice in the education of its children.

The report cards were distributed and the result tallied. Along with over four hundred of the actual report cards, a summary of the principal's grades was sent to him.

As a second strategy, unidentified members of the community decided to engage in a bit of creative multiculturalism. They took down the cutouts of Anglo children in the hall and replaced them with blown-up photographs of successful graduates of the school. The principal immediately removed the new posters, not because it was a bad idea, he said, but because he had not authorized their placement.

At a public meeting the principal decided to assert his authority. He declared that parents would no longer be allowed in the building during school hours. When community activists confronted him, he refused to respond since they weren't parents. When parents then took up the argument, he called the meeting to an end. But as people were leaving the building, the principal was overheard talking to his assistant by several parents and activists. He said something to the effect that parents were ignorant, uncivilized, and easily swayed by radicals. Moreover, he said, many of them were not good Christians and brought primitive beliefs such as voodoo from Mexico. His comments revealed not merely his cultural and geographic ignorance but his fear of the community as well. For the next several weeks the principal received anonymous packages in the mail, both at home and at school. They contained strange-smelling powders and potions, chicken parts, cotton doused in what looked like blood, and fingernail clippings. When he called the police, he was told not to worry. He asked parents what all this meant and got no response. Soon he began to suffer from insomnia and was afraid to walk the halls of school alone. Within weeks he had decided to take early retirement and was replaced immediately with a Mexican-American principal. In any case, the community had spoken both subtly and directly to the former principal, showing him how they really felt about his Eurocentric disrespect for their children. Though some problems certainly remained, a step toward greater equity had been taken.

These are not strategies I'd necessarily recommend, but they do illustrate how ignorance pervades monocultural thinking and by implication the curriculum that embodies it. The story illustrates to what lengths we sometimes have to go in the name of our children and their dignity. This is a sad commentary on how far we are from being a society with high regard for equity, though it is encouraging to know that occasionally the antic spirit emerges triumphant in the struggle for multiculturalism and simple fairness.

It is important, however, to go beyond mere harassment and defensive struggle. There are many different forms that the struggle for equity can take. One is to write about it; to paraphrase the title of Ishmael Reed's recent book of essays, writing is a form of fighting.

Another way is to reconstruct the curriculum and demystify what I call the "excellence demagogues." These are the experts who claim that quality and excellence is their territory and that multiculturalism is at best a secondary enrichment of the curriculum, at worst a dilution of the substance of education for all children. These are people who would substitute historical misrepresentation, cultural chauvinism, and the poverty of majoritarian narrative for the richness of multicultural learning.

A somewhat sophisticated example of this attitude was the proclamation printed in large type across the front of a pamphlet for a seminar on "the arts in the schools": "We need to study Western Cultures to understand our past. We need to study non-Western cultures to understand our future."

This quote, attributed to Ernest Boyer of the Carnegie Foundation for the Advancement of Teaching, might be loosely paraphrased this way: "We, the white Americans, need to study a romanticized version of West European cultures such as Germany, France, and England, excepting most of the Mediterranean countries and Eastern Europe other than where and when they fit into our notion of the Glory that was Greece and the Splendor that was Rome, but not including contemporary Italy and Greece. The reason for this is to understand the superior values built into these interpretations of our white presumed past and to continue to fight for our dominance over the rest of the world. We also need to study non-Western and especially Asian cultures to understand our future since they are getting too powerful for their own good and we will have to confront them about this in the future."

The norming of excellence, by now standard practice in schools, usually goes unnoticed. One battle we must all fight is the reconstruction of the content of learning and the redefinition of excellence. This means that the notion of excellence will not be based on any one culture but will be tied to the quality of work within a multiplicity of traditions. We must find a way to help our children see our collective history from many perspectives and to understand that oppression does not provide the same experience for the oppressed as it does for the oppressor. We must also open children's eyes to the wonder of difference, to help them recognize the imaginative genius of all peoples.

Teachers do not have to do this by themselves. We must once again become students ourselves, learning to teach in new ways with new perspectives. Scholars in all fields of study are constructing multiple narratives and creating for us new vocabularies and understandings. In the case of the literature of African-American people, we must read authors like Henry Louis Gates, Jr., and integrate into our daily life his insights and those of his colleagues. Gates describes, in the context of black literature, what I am talking about for the literatures of the world and for learning in general:

> . . . to theorize about black literatures, we must do what all theorists do. And that is to read the texts that comprise our literary tradition, formulate (by reasoning from observed facts) useful principles of criticism from within that textual tradition, then draw upon these to read the texts that make up that tradition. . . . *All* theorists do this and we must as well. . . . My position is that for a critic of black literature to borrow European or American theories of literature regardless of *"where they come from"* is for that critic to be trapped in a relation of intellectual indenture or colonialism. . . . One must know one's textual terrain before it can be explored; one must know one's literary tradition before it can be theorized about. . . . To discourage us from reading our own texts in ways suggested by those very texts is to encourage new forms of neocolonialism.*

---

*Henry Louis Gates, Jr., "Talkin' That Truth" in *"Race," Writing, and Difference* (Chicago: University of Chicago Press, 1986), p. 406.

We must enter other worlds of literature, imagination, and culture in order to enrich ourselves and inform our teaching. This enrichment is at the heart of excellence and is the core of equity. The two are inseparable. As hard as it is to relearn what we thought we knew, we have no other responsible choice.

Uncommon Differences
On Political Correctness, Core Curriculum,
and Democracy in Education

I FIRST HEARD THE phrase "politically correct" in the late 1940s and early 1950s in reference to the political debates between socialists and members of the United States Communist Party (CP). These debates were an everyday occurrence in my neighborhood in the Bronx until the McCarthy committee and the House Un-American Activities Committee silenced political talk on the streets. Members of the CP talked about current party doctrine as the "correct" line for the moment. During World War II the Hitler-Stalin pact caused many CP members considerable pain and often disgrace on my block, which was all Jewish and mostly socialist. The "correct" position on Stalin's alliance with Hitler was considered to be ridiculous, a betrayal of European Jewry as well as socialist ideas. The term "politically correct" was used disparagingly to refer to someone whose loyalty to the CP line overrode compassion and led to bad politics. It was used by socialists against Communists, and was meant to separate out socialists, who believed in egalitarian moral ideas, from dogmatic Communists, who would advocate and defend party positions regardless of their moral substance.

Given that history, it was surprising to hear right-wing intellectuals in the 1990s using the phrase "politically correct" to disparage students and professors who advocate multiculturalism and are willing to confront racism, sexism, or homophobia at the university. Yet it is not uncommon, for example, for right-wing critics to accuse students (or other professors) who insist that women's voices or the voices of people of color be included in the curriculum of making rigid, oppressive demands that infringe upon academic freedom. The implication of these accusations is that people calling for compliance with antisexist and antiracist education today are similar to the Communist party hard-liners who insisted on compliance with the "correct" line on the Hitler-Stalin pact. It is a clever ploy on the part of neoconservatives, a number of whom were former CP members and know how the phrase "politically correct" was used in the past, to insinuate that egalitarian democratic ideas are actually authoritarian, orthodox, and Communist-influenced when they oppose the right of people to be racist, sexist, and homophobic. The accusation of being "politically correct" is a weapon used by right-wing professors, and publicized by conservative media critics, to protect themselves against criticisms of their own biases by students or other, usually younger, professors. It is a way of diverting the issue of bias within the university to issues of freedom of speech without acknowledging that the right to question professorial authority is also a free-speech matter.

There is a major question about whether professors have a right, within the framework of academic classes where they control students' grades and therefore students' future options, to be racist, sexist, and culturally biased when expressing those ideas in class is likely to disrupt the learning process. The question is whether the classroom, in which students and professors are not equals, can become a bully pulpit for racist and sexist ideologies as much as it is an issue of academic freedom or freedom of speech. After all, the classroom is not a free-speech forum where equals gather to express opinions. It is a site of judgment as much as a place of learning, where professors judge their students as much as educate them. Academic freedom is equivalent, in this context, to professorial control of ideas, not to free speech. I remember, for example, the control of legitimacy exerted by philosophy professors when I was at Harvard in the 1950s. At that time Sartre, Merleau-Ponty, Heidegger, and just about all the continental European philosophers were ridiculed and their works put off-limits. Any student who took existentialism, phenomenology, or Marxism seriously, for example, was advised to find another major. Only British analytic philosophy, logic, and the philosophy of mathematics were considered intellectually respectable. At that time even the works of Wittgenstein were suspect for being too mystical and unclear. If students tried, as I sometimes did, to question their professors' preferences, they were punished both through their grades and through the kinds of recommendations they got. Philosophical correctness governed learning in the department. The professors' academic freedom to control content and discourse in their fields of expertise limited their students' intellectual freedom.

As I see it, the academic-freedom issue these days is being used to mask the desire of neoconservatives to exert control over ideas at the university and push out ethnic and women's studies as well as prevent the rethinking of the curriculum from a world rather than a West European perspective. In this light the defenders of academic freedom are the ones who are taking a rigid, "correct" line and trying to shut up students and other professors who are proclaiming that there are fundamental problems about the way universities have traditionally defined what it is necessary to know in order to be an educated person.

Right-wing professors who challenge students' rights to question racist and sexist attitudes and opinions seem to be effective at the postsecondary level. However, the Right has not yet been able to shift the debates in public schools from the fundamental equity and equality issues to issues of academic freedom and the personal freedom of expression. There are a number of reasons for this, among which is the fact that the students in most public schools, in urban centers at least, are predominantly minority, the majority of teachers are women, and the expression of racist and sexist ideas are, by consensus, agreed to be out of place and counter to the educational process. This context for considering ethnic and cultural issues and women's issues is very different from the context of overwhelmingly white college student bodies with predominantly white male faculties. Those are not the only reasons, however, that the accusation of political correctness has not surfaced in the schools in the same form that it has at the university. Another important reason this shift from issues of equity to issues of free expression has not been made in the schools is that teachers and college professors do not lead the same professional lives or have the same latitudes of freedom within their jobs.

Teachers work five days a week, eight hours a day during the school year. They are required to be with their students during all teaching hours and are not allowed to leave their classes unsupervised. They are assigned grade and subject levels and, within the constraints of their credentials, can be involuntarily transferred from grade to grade, subject to subject, and even school to school. Most often they are required to teach a set curriculum mandated at the local-school district, or state level. In addition, they are expected to keep their personal politics and values out of the classroom and are subject to parental and community as well as administrative scrutiny.

Classroom teachers have levels of control imposed on them that professors would appropriately consider to be assaults on their academic freedom and insults to their professional expertise. These levels range from immediate site administration to district-level scrutiny as well as outside, university-based evaluation. Beyond these there are state commissions of education that mandate standards and curriculum content. Within these systems of constraint teachers have developed a covert social code that prohibits outspoken disagreement about educational ideas on a faculty level. Just about everyone complies. Those who don't are usually given the silent treatment during the school year and then involuntarily transferred. I know the power of this code, having been a victim of it years ago as a first-year teacher who tried to speak out about racism at my school and found myself involuntarily transferred to another school. I have also seen some of my current student teachers punished in the same way, just last year.

The individual freedom to express unpopular or even new ideas in the classroom is controlled for both student and teacher by a system that marginalizes such behavior as deviant, disobedient, and "political." Even though there are occasional individual protests and even some successes, it is only when a protest becomes a collective and public matter that systemwide changes develop. Thus, so far as I can tell, the issue of political correctness does not exist within the elementary and secondary schools because there is little protest about racist and sexist practices from within a school. Individuals and small groups who oppose the traditional norms of public schools are simply shuffled around or thrown out. The attempt by individuals to change the norms and values of the institution, even if those norms and values are racist and sexist, is treated as no greater threat in the case of gender, ethnicity, and culture than in the case of budget, supplies, and class size. As an individual teacher or student, for example, it is very difficult to confront a racist teacher at your own school. The individual teacher will be accused of breaking ranks and being disloyal to the teaching profession and will be subsequently isolated or transferred. The student will be defined as disruptive and sent to a special-education class.

Threats to the public schools are, however, taken seriously when they come from outside of the individual school—from community groups, teachers' unions, central administrators, university-based experts, the media, and state departments of education. Teaching within the public schools is considered a social act that has to be responsible to societal forces, whereas teaching at the university is still within the domain of individual professorial control within the context of self-certifying professions.

Even though issues of equality, equity, and multicultural-ism—which are at the heart of debates about political correct-ness—are not played out on an individual level within the public schools, they are being confronted on the much larger scale of institutional and public policy. Those forces that keep the indi-vidual teacher powerless and the individualistic problem of politi-cal correctness out of the public schools are the same forces that are central to overt debates about affirmative action, multicultural curriculum, and gender-fair education. Public schools may pre-tend to a mythology of political neutrality and have built-in mech-anisms of control, but because they have the obligation to accept all of the children, they must respond to the communities they serve. Given that the public schools in most cities in the United States are predominantly nonwhite, that, for example, whites make up a minority of public school students in the state of California and may be close to that status nationwide, the schools must deal with multiculturalism and racism. And since the schools, as opposed to the colleges and universities, are predomi-nantly staffed by women, they must also deal with issues of gender and sexism. It is one thing for a few professors at the University of Michigan to defend their cultural and gender biases in such an overwhelmingly white institution and another to defend the same attitudes toward culture and gender in the New York City public school system, where fewer than 20 percent of the students are white and over 68 percent of the teachers are women.

As a practical matter, the political forces for equity and equal-ity are stronger within the community of people concerned about public education than within the community of people concerned about colleges and universities. To continue to teach the superiority of white European male-dominated culture in schools where 90 to 100 percent of the students are African-American, Asian-American, or Latino, for example, is not merely to perpetuate unsubstantiated myths, but to insult the culture and integrity of the students and the community, and to insult the gender, competence, and quality of the majority of the teachers. It causes teachers to lose credibility with their students and within the school's community and puts teachers in the role of defending a dying colonialism that is considered the enemy of learning by students, parents, and community members alike.

Even a neoconservative educator like Diane Ravitch must come up with some concessions to multiculturalism in the school curriculum to maintain credibility in the debate over the content of public education. She sets herself firmly on the ground of supporting a West European curriculum with multicultural add-ons, a position that, at Stanford and other universities, which modified their freshman civilization courses to include non-Western sources, would be considered by neoconservatives to favor the undermining of Western civilization. In the schools, however, that position is conservative and opposed by advocates of ethnocentric and pluralistic curriculums that place Eurocentric visions of history and culture in the perspective of many other cultural visions. In Portland, Oregon, for example, the entire school district has adopted an Afrocentric, multicultural curriculum that treats the history and culture of the United States from the perspective of all of the peoples that made our nation. This is not merely a minor change in focus, but a fundamental rethinking of what we tell our children about who we are as a society.

Let me give an example of Eurocentric curriculum and show why it has been rejected in many public school systems. The Addison-Wesley high school textbook *United States History from 1865*, volume 2 (1986), summarizes U.S. history from "prehistory to 1850" in pages 4 to 31. African-American peoples enter the stage of U.S. history on page 8 in the following words: "Traders also exchanged New England rum in Africa for slaves to be sold in the West Indies or the Thirteen Colonies." Aside from the historical falsity of the assertion that rum was the sole medium of exchange in the slave trade and its racist implications for current debates on substance abuse, there is the question of people being introduced as slaves. Were they slaves or were they carpenters, kings, weavers, farmers, etc., who were stolen into slavery? Whose perspective do we want our children to take?

The textbook destroys black people's identity by starting from slavery, rather than from Africa prior to slavery. It is centered on the perceptions and narratives of slave masters, not the people who are their victims. It gives students no sense of the language, culture, and society of the people who were made slaves, and therefore encourages the idea that enslaved Africans came to this continent with nothing to offer other than involuntary labor and the ability to breed. If this seems like an exaggeration, I suggest you go into a white middle-class school that uses such texts and ask the students about the character and culture of early African arrivals on this continent.

The textbook I am using for an example does, however, make concessions to multiculturalism, as Ravitch would advocate. For example, the same page I quoted above has a large sidebar devoted to the life of Olaudah Equiano. His story begins when he was enslaved at eleven. Nothing before. Then we are told about nice whites who rescued him from slavery and are given a full color picture of the galley of a slave ship. The reader can take nothing away from this multicultural pastiche other than that Equiano was a slave, that slavery was horrible, and that he was rescued through the kind graces of whites. Where is his person, his culture, his humanity?

It is personhood, culture, and humanity that Afrocentric and other ethnocentric curricula try to provide, as well as more historical truth than is allowed in our history textbooks. There are unpleasant aspects of our national history, and it is better for our children to know about them than to become party to reproducing them.

Recently, the textbook-adoption committees in Oakland and Hayward, California, rejected all social studies books that came before them for consideration. The grounds were that without exception they were racist, sexist, and historically inaccurate. The state textbook-adoption committee in California accepted only one series. That series was adopted as the best of a bad lot simply because school people claimed that most schools could not function without textbooks. There were some of us, however, who suggested it was better to go without texts for a few years and rewrite the texts, which is what Oakland and Hayward decided to do.

The textbook wars in California make university-based struggles to add a few books to Western culture classes seem mild. And that is only part of the rethinking of the content of school curricula that is currently taking place. Women's groups are increasingly vocal about the representation of females throughout the curriculum; other groups are making school people more sensitive to slights and insults on the basis of handicaps, age, or sexual orientation. Many teachers are listening and, because they have support outside of their schools, they are taking leadership roles in making the schools more democratic and decent places for all children. Of course, there is resistance, but not as much as in the universities. That is because white dominance is slipping in the arena of public education. Unfortunately, with that slippage, we see a strategy of defending public education, breaking up public school systems through bogus choice programs, and official neglect.

I believe the culture wars in the public schools reveal the issues that underline the media events that constitute the political correctness debate. These issues are not about professors' rights to freedom of speech in their classrooms but are struggles over shifts in dominance in our society. They represent resistance to demands for multicultural and gender-fair inclusive curricula.

E. D. Hirsch, Jr., under the guise of proposing a core curriculum for all students from first through sixth grades, has mounted a subtle attack on multiculturalism, and on antisexist and antiracist curriculum. Hirsch, you may remember, is the author of the best-selling book *Cultural Literacy*, which is subtitled *What every American needs to know*. At the end of that book Hirsch provides a sixty-three-page list of words and phrases that "illustrate the character and range of the knowledge literate Americans tend to share."* That list provides the language and conceptual apparatus of Hirsch's vision of "Everyman," a university-educated European American, most likely male, who speaks in platitudes and has a passing acquaintance with words drawn from the sciences, humanities, and the arts. For example, Hirsch's Everyman tends to "know" the following *P* words and phrases:

> perfectibility of man, periodic table of the elements, pax Romana, pay the piper, pearl of great price, peeping Tom, Peloponnesian War, penis envy, penny saved is a penny earned, persona non grata, Peter the Great, Phi Beta Kappa, philosopher king, photoelectric cell, plate tectonics, Pickwickian, Planck's constant, play second fiddle, pogrom, proof of the pudding is in the eating, and Pyrrhic victory.†

I've been searching for Hirsch's Everyman and haven't found anyone who knows all of the words on this very abbreviated list. "Planck's constant" stumps just about everybody. An equal number are uncertain about the exact nature of "photoelectric cells" and "plate tectonics." "Perfectibility of man" and the "periodic table" are recognized but not necessarily understood in any complex way. "Peter the Great" and the "Peloponnesian War" are

---

* (Boston: Houghton Mifflin, 1987), p. 146.

† From pp. 193–98.

somewhat more familiar, though the "pax Romana" is often greeted by a blank stare.

The people I asked are all college-educated, quite well read, and are interested in ideas. They are not college professors, and their work does not involve constant reference and citation. However, by any reasonable definition of "literate," they qualify. Where they part ways with Hirsch's list is in areas where special knowledge is required or an archaic, Latinate, and formal way of speaking is implied.

Perhaps there are people who have mastered the meaning of most of the words on the list and understand the concepts they represent in some depth, and it may be that Hirsch wishes to restrict his notion of literacy to that small group of polymaths. He seems, however, to include among the literate those people who have encountered the words on the list at one time or another during their reading or education and only have a vague idea of what many of them mean. The problem is that Hirsch elevates such superficial acquaintance with words to the status of "knowledge." That is why, when he turns to learning in the early grades, he can take a strong stand in favor of rote learning and the memorization of factual information, while insisting that "all children master a core of information that is necessary to their competence as learners in later grades."* Mastery, for Hirsch, is memorization; information is knowledge. Parents must, he says, "decline to be bullied by oversimplified slogans (like 'learning to learn') which have not worked."† Hirsch argues that mastery of what he calls core knowledge is a necessary step we must take in the United States toward creating fairness and excellence in education:

---

* *What Your First Grader Needs to Know: Fundamentals of a Good First Grade Education* (Garden City, N.Y.: Doubleday, 1991), p. 10.

† Ibid.

In this period of our national life, to ensure that all young children possess a core of shared knowledge is a fundamental reform that, while not sufficient by itself to achieve excellence and fairness in schooling, is nonetheless a *necessary* [italics added] step in developing a first-rate educational system in the United States.*

Hirsch's core of knowledge is derived from an idealized construction of European history which implies that it is a manifestation of all that is excellent in the history of humankind. In defining what is central there is much that Hirsch chooses to leave out. As pointed out in Graywolf Press's anthology, *Multicultural Literacy*,† which criticizes Hirsch for his Eurocentric cultural bias, Hirsch's list leaves out many words and phrases that relate to progressive thinking and non-Western culture. Among the *P*'s, for example, Hirsch's sixty-three-page list has overlooked words and phrases such as

peace activists, pesticides, political prisoners, potlatch, premenstrual syndrome, prison, prophylactic, prostitution, pueblo, and prime time.

Whatever one's conception of a culturally literate adult, it can reasonably be assumed that most of these concepts are as central to the "core" in our culture as ones on Hirsch's list. It is difficult not to wonder how Hirsch's list is generated and what justification he has to decide upon the legislation of a core of knowledge, given the complexity of life and language in our society. The question of who decides what is core knowledge becomes even more crucial in the case of legislating a "necessary" curriculum for young children.

The list of omissions drawn from *Multicultural Literacy* can easily be expanded, and Hirsch would most likely respond by adding some of the above omitted words to his core list while

---

* Ibid., p. 2.

† Rick Simonson and Scott Walker, *Multicultural Literacy* (Minneapolis: Graywolf Press, 1988).

arguing for cultural literacy as an expanding process with a Euro-centric core. However, in addition to this amended list there are other words and phrases that so-called literate Americans "tend" to know, words and phrases such as

> prick, piss, putz, pussy, patronize, palimony, prissy, putsch, pig (as in violent police officer, as opposed to "pig in a poke, buy a," which is on Hirsch's list), profligate, play politics, play the field, poke fun at, play into one's hands, and pick apart.

Hirsch does not acknowledge that these words contribute to making a literate person. Literacy is a morally correct notion for Hirsch, one that distinguishes between what is proper and what is not. Hirsch has selected part of a so-called literate person's whole vocabulary and chosen to elevate that as "literate." Yet, who can read and comprehend much of the best in Western literature without understanding the "low" list as well as Hirsch's "high" list? Hirsch may be pure, but literature isn't.

There are real problems with the cultural and class biases of the notion of cultural literacy that Hirsch is selling. There are also problems with his notion of what knowledge is. All of this goes to the heart of why his new books for parents and teachers, with the pretentious titles *What Your First Grader Needs to Know: Fundamentals of a Good First Grade Education* and *What Your Second Grader Needs to Know: Fundamentals of a Good Second Grade Education*, are pernicious, stupid, and dangerous. These two books are the first of six volumes published by Doubleday, one for each grade from the first through the sixth, which constitute the *Core Knowledge Series*.* The six volumes prescribe "a specific sequence of core knowledge that young Americans should at a minimum learn."† There is no modesty involved in Hirsch's claim for the importance of this series. According to him, teach-

---

* Garden City, N.Y.: Doubleday, 1991.

† From the general introduction included in all volumes of the series, p. 1.

ing the sequence laid out in the series is "a *necessary* [italics added] step in developing a first-rate educational system in the United States."* Hirsch even goes on to point out that "all of the best—i.e., highest-achieving and most egalitarian—school systems in the world, such as those in Sweden, France, and Japan, teach their children a specific core of knowledge in each of the first six grades" and that "shared background knowledge makes schooling more fair and democratic."† In addition, "shared background knowledge helps create cooperation and solidarity in school and nation."‡ Indeed, according to Hirsch, "no modern nation has achieved both excellence and fairness in education without defining core knowledge for the elementary school."§

First off, Hirsch begs the central question of whether any "modern nation" has achieved either excellence or fairness in education, and does not bother to substantiate his claims about Japan, France, and Sweden. Of his three examples, Japan and France have elitist school systems that do not have a universal postsecondary education as a goal. Competition to enter the elite schools in those systems is intense, test-related, and frequently class-bound. Immigrant communities in both societies, but especially in France, are for the most part out of the system, and racism, both personal and institutional, is not uncommon in their schools.

But there are other problems with Hirsch's call for a national core curriculum. First of all, when talking about adult literacy, Hirsch lists what literate Americans "tend" to know and have as shared knowledge. However, when he comes to children, he strengthens his position to claiming that he provides a curriculum of what children "need to" know. There is quite a bit of slippage

---

* Ibid., p. 2.

† Ibid., pp. 2, 3.

‡ Ibid., p. 4.

§ Ibid., p. 5.

between "tends to" and "needs to." What one tends to know can be derived from many different sources, and the overlap of one person's knowledge with that of others is a matter of experience, cultural background, gender, and class. What one "needs" to know becomes a matter of prescription and, if one considers the movement toward a national curriculum, even legislation. At the core of Hirsch's program for young children is a desire to set a path from childhood through adolescence that will channel young people's thinking. However, even if he succeeds in legislating his core curriculum, I believe that Hirsch's enterprise is bound to fail to provide either the quality educational system or the production of excellence in learning he claims for it.

It is important to look at the notion of core knowledge itself and understand the contradictions built into it in order to understand that it is a formula for failure as well as an insult to the intelligence of the children it presumes to educate. One way to begin is to look at Hirsch's first- and second-grade books and examine what he considers required knowledge for six- and seven-year-olds.

The books themselves are designed to look like old school texts. They are drab, badly illustrated, and not meant to charm or interest children. In fact, the reading level of the books is much too difficult for beginning readers. The books are meant to be read to children, not read by them. The child is to receive knowledge from the books as mediated by some adult, not to participate in her or his own learning. From the very beginning, Hirsch sets up a situation in which the child is to accept whatever is prescribed rather than learn to question and explore issues and ideas.

Within this passive learning situation Hirsch offers six- and seven-year-olds nursery rhymes, fairy tales, proverbs, music lessons, history, science, and math—all that is presumably *necessary* to succeed in school. The connection between later school success and mastery of this material is never made, and yet, that claim is used as a selling point in advertisement for the books. The whole enterprise smacks of the same advertising hype which claims that expensive cars will lead to sexual success and fancy speakers will result in heightened self-esteem.

The reason particular rhymes and tales were included in the books and others omitted is baffling. Some of Hirsch's choices seem bizarre, like having a section entitled "Patriotic Music" as part of necessary learning in the second grade. The two books, read straight through, seem like hastily pasted together collections of platitudes and pieties, part McGuffey's reader and part nineteenth-century math and science exercise books.

An examination of some of the specific contents of Hirsch's core curriculum raises some serious educational questions that go beyond style and hype, however. First- and second-graders, according to Hirsch, must know, in order to succeed in the future, *Cinderella, Sleeping Beauty, Hansel and Gretel, Beauty and the Beast, The Princess and the Pea,* and *Snow White,* among other tales. If children don't know these, they are likely to fail as they move through elementary school and high school, according to Hirsch. Why? We are never told, but I suppose it's because if they can take in those tales as exemplary, they can take in anything the authorities want to shove down their throats. These tales of royalty and wealth are filled with passive or wicked females, evil stepparents, pure and handsome princes, or kind, innocent, and harried fathers. Young women are portrayed as needing to be rescued from older women, purified for marriage into royalty, or sacrificed to save their fathers. In *Snow White,* for example, we have a wicked but beautiful stepmother who tries to murder her stepdaughter. The reason for all this seems to be that the stepmother (for whom there is no sympathy whatever in the tale) is getting older and becomes aware that her stepdaughter, Snow White, is beginning to surpass her in beauty. Because the only power accorded to both Snow White and her stepmother is their physical beauty, and because aging is inevitable, the tale becomes an implacable and murderous encounter between generations of women. In fact, in the original Grimm version, when the prince decides to take Snow White as his bride, the stepmother is invited to the wedding. A surprise is awaiting her at the celebration:

> And when she (the stepmother) went in she recognized Snow-White; and she stood still with rage and fear, and could not stir. But iron slippers had already been put on the fire, and they were brought in with tongs, and set before her. Then she was forced to put on the red-hot shoes, and dance until she dropped dead.*

This is the gruesome conclusion to a tale our children *need* to know in order to succeed in school. The central problem here and one that is at the root of creating any core knowledge is that it will not be taken in the same way by all learners—there is no core response. For some, especially the want-to-be princes in the classes, it can be an affirming and empowering tale. For others, the girls who believe in their autonomy and refuse to accept male definitions of their strengths, it can be disconfirming. For stepchildren, it can reinforce family tension. For children who do not see themselves as European princes and princesses, it can lead to depression and marginalize their participation. And for all children it can provide a model of cruel and vindictive revenge that might allow them to tolerate or even contribute to the sufferings of others.

The nature of this story is to categorize and divide people, to judge them by externals, and to reinforce an order in which upper-class-male power makes all the rules. This is not necessary knowledge for children in a democracy, though as one story among a thousand, if learned in a casual setting, it probably wouldn't cause much damage.

Even Hirsch, or the people who actually wrote the text of the tales in his books, acknowledge some aspects of the problematic

---

* *The Complete Grimm's Fairy Tales* (New York: Pantheon, 1972), p. 258.

nature of this tale, for Grimm's ending of *Snow White* is softened by Hirsch's version:

> As for the wicked Queen, some say she fell off a cliff, some say she was struck by lightning, and some say she danced herself to death at Snow White's wedding. But one thing is certain: she never bothered Snow White again, and Snow White and the prince lived happily ever after.*

Grimm has no "happily ever after" and is unambiguous about the fate of the queen. Hirsch has reconstructed his core for a gentler and kinder America. So our core knowledge, in Hirsch's hands, is not even authentic. Rather, it is a moralistic manipulation of traditional materials that purges them of the cruelty and bias that is part of the European heritage and which determines many of the ways in which people in the United States treat each other.

Hirsch claims that a common core of knowledge creates fairness in education. Nazi Germany had a core curriculum, as did the Stalinist Soviet Union. It elevates the values of the people who legislate that core to the status of universal standards of excellence; but if the core reproduces the inequities that exist in a society, it is simply another attempt to keep power relations from changing.

The covert text of Hirsch's core curriculum implies that no fundamental economic or social changes need occur to create equity (he uses the word "fairness") in education and that sensitivity to children's knowledge about their own life circumstances is irrelevant to the educational process. For example, another proverb Hirsch would require all six-year-olds to know is "There's no place like home," adding the following commentary that parents and teachers are urged to share with children: "People use this saying to mean: travel may be pleasant, but home is the best place of all. 'We had a great trip, but there's no place like home.' "† Try sharing this with a group of children living in the

---

First Grader, p. 54.

† *First Grader*, p. 81.

midst of violence and poverty—tell them that the proverb provides necessary knowledge for them to succeed in school, and ask them to share their travels and describe how wonderful it felt when they got home. Add insult to the injury of poverty in the name of fairness, deny middle-class bias in the curriculum, and you have hard-core Hirsch.

To be sure, there are some concessions to diversity and multiculturalism in Hirsch's volumes. In the first-grade volume, out of twenty tales there is one from Africa, one of Spanish origin (not Latin-American, however), and one Native American tale. In the stories of great scientists there are one European male (Copernicus), one American female (Rachel Carson), and one African-American male (Charles Drew). One wonders: why these three? But there is even more of a problem within this effort at showing diversity. Consider the following quote from the minibiography of Charles Drew, whose scientific work was responsible for making blood transfusions easy and who set up the first blood bank. Also remember that this is supposed to be part of necessary knowledge for all six-year-olds.

> For a long time, the Army and Navy refused to accept blood from black people. Even after it started to accept "colored" blood, the Army told the Red Cross to separate the donated blood of black people from that of whites. Charles Drew explained that there was no such thing as "black" and "white" blood. Blood was blood. But no one listened. This made Charles Drew very sad and angry. He resigned from the Red Cross.*

So we know that Charles Drew was sad and angry. The army spoke to the Red Cross. No one listened to scientific evidence. But in this version there are no specific white people involved, no racism, no ignorance or rejection of science. There is no rage.

---

* *First Grader*, p. 233.

What is this telling children about Drew? That he got sad and quit. So what happened then? Was there a confrontation? Did Drew do more than quit? According to the *Historical and Cultural Atlas of African Americans* by Molefi K. Asante and Mark T. Mattson,

> the importance of Charles Drew's research was underscored by the fact that Europe was at war [World War I] . . . and thousands of soldiers who would have been considered mortally wounded prior to Dr. Drew's discoveries, were saved. In 1941 the American Red Cross appointed Drew director of its first Blood Bank. When Pearl Harbor was attacked by the Japanese, Drew was able to provide blood plasma for Americans who were wounded during the surprise attack.
>
> However, the American Red Cross decided to use only blood from white donors for wounded members of the military, insisting that they did not want to mix the blood of African Americans with white blood. Drew was enraged. He resigned from his position over the unscientific position of the American Red Cross saying, "The blood of individual human beings may differ by blood type groupings, but there is absolutely no scientific basis to indicate any difference according to race."*

According to *Webster's American Biographies*, "instead of establishing a private practice, he spent his time in teaching and recruiting" African Americans to become doctors.†

Drew died in an automobile accident at the age of forty-six. According to the *Historical and Cultural Atlas of African Americans*:

> On April 1, 1950 . . . [Drew] was fatally injured in a car accident in North Carolina. . . . It was reported that Drew bled to death because

---

* (New York: Macmillan, 1991), pp. 136–37.

† (Springfield, Mass.: G. & C. Merriam, 1975), p. 292.

the "white" hospital would not admit him. Ironically, the surgeon, scientist, scholar, whose life's work was devoted to saving others was denied access to the methods and procedures he invented to save his own life.*

If we choose to tell our children about Charles Drew (a fine thing to do, though perhaps not a necessity for six-year-olds), we owe them a story that does justice to Drew's pain and to his reaction to racism as well as his brilliance. It might help them understand more about how racism functions and how it can be confronted. Since six-year-olds can be victims of racism or can perpetuate it, there is no reason why they shouldn't also be helped to think about it. This points once again to the danger of avoiding dealing with the processes by which learning takes place and believing, as Hirsch seems to do, that the only important thing is the information learned.

Hirsch insists that the information contained in his core curriculum, and not the way it is taught or how students respond to or think about it, is what will provide fairness in the curriculum. He defends rote learning. And yet even rote learning isn't as simple as Hirsch makes it out to be. To memorize and regurgitate something that is humiliating or insulting, to preserve in your memory as received authority disempowering stories, partial truths, and homilies that go against your better judgment or insult your experience, is not a road to fairness or excellence but rather a sure formula for the perpetuation of ignorance and inequality.

Hirsch's books are dangerous because they have been packaged to provide anxious parents and nervous educators with a formulaic road to competitive advantage. Despite mouthing the idea that they provide a fair basis for all children to get ahead in school, they implicitly promise that if your child does master the content they provide, she or he will get ahead in school. However, by raising the question of core knowledge and its relationship to

---

* *Historical and Cultural Atlas*, p. 137.

critical thinking in the context of schools, Hirsch has done us a favor. Those of us who believe that learning is more than memorization must also examine the question of what should be the core content of a curriculum that promotes democratic thinking and gives children tools and understanding that will help them confront inequity as they try to make a decent life for themselves. It is not enough to be concerned with process and to focus exclusively on critical analysis, experiential learning, personal sensitivity, and creative expression, as some progressive educators do. As educators we must also examine what knowledge our students need to have in order to survive and thrive. Surely at some point they must learn the Bill of Rights—not merely memorize it as Hirsch might have it, but know intimately the ways in which those rights are theirs and the ways in which they must be defended or be lost. They must know the Constitution, critically, but section by section as well. They must also know enough of our common history and creative life to be able to place themselves in the whole. How much content must be contained in the core and when it should be taught is a difficult but necessary question for us to confront. That it should be taught critically and with a respect for the student's person and thoughts as well as for differences in culture, gender and class, is beyond question for me. Process and content must be merged into a thoughtful and critical pedagogy. Moreover, we must go beyond this common core and consider other cores of knowledge that are essential for specific groups of students. Girls and young women must learn women's history; African-American youngsters must learn history from the perspective of the strengths of their people. The same is true of Latino, Asian, and European-American students. All students must become comfortable with multiple narratives—their own and other peoples'. As educators, we must move toward creating a common composite narrative that approximates the complex and too often painful history of our nation. Fairness in education can only emerge from such diversity.

Just as we as a nation are still struggling to achieve a democratic society, we as educators are still struggling to understand what education in a democracy should look like. To settle on a core curriculum, as Hirsch is trying to do, is inherently unjust. To eliminate content and focus solely on critical process is to foolishly deny the importance of knowledge, history, and literature. The struggle to weigh process and knowledge in a way that respects the diversity of our society and counters the inequities that are perpetuated through schooling is perhaps the central unaddressed question of current debates about educational reform. What we might come up with is a continually emerging and self-renewing curriculum, with a constantly evolving and shifting core and a critique informed by student voices and the voices of their communities—that is, with a curriculum that is part of the struggle to make a democracy out of the United States.

It is important for people who are concerned with making sense of the debates about political correctness at colleges and universities to look at the debates about curriculum content in the schools. Expressing racist and sexist ideas to children is not looked upon as harmless, neutral, and a matter of a teacher's academic freedom. Imagine a person who preaches racism to first- and second-graders trying to defend that stance by accusing parents and school district personnel of limiting his or her academic freedom. Imagine the same teacher accusing parents and community members of rigid political correctness because they refuse to allow their children to be exposed to racist and sexist ideas. If the issue weren't so serious, the person would be laughed at. It is damaging to students, insulting to communities, unprofessional, and immoral to be teaching racism or sexism to children.

What is pejoratively called "political correctness" by academic reactionaries at universities is simply considered to be morally right and personally sensitive in the context of public schools. It is in the public schools where we are most likely to see major changes in sensitivity and awareness over issues of race, ethnicity, and gender. It is also where university educators should look for models of a broader, more democratic, though equally demanding, curriculum that provides an accurate account of what our society has been and a vision of what it might become if its democratic ideals are taken seriously.

Creative Maladjustment and the Struggle for Public Education

Iᴛ ɪs ᴠᴇʀʏ difficult for me to throw out things that evoke memories or stories and so, over the last thirty years, I have amassed a collection of my students' writing and art. Recently I came upon a portfolio of pastels done by children in my first public school class in 1962. There was Sara's delicate copy of a Modigliani portrait, done in browns and oranges; a blue and white drawing of Moby Dick jumping out of the sea, done by Hugh Lee on black construction paper; a hand with an evil eye, drawn by Carlos M.; and Gloria's frightening lion's face with knife slashes all over it, whose title, "All cut up," is written in red crayon over the pastel.

I remember buying the pastels for my class and letting the students draw, paint, or sketch all afternoon. They could also play chess, dominoes, and checkers, read with me, write poems and books, or listen to music and build clay models if they cared to. Those afternoon activities were my way of warding off chaos and, at the same time, getting to know and occasionally help my students personally. It took me a while to realize that these activities were not diversions but at the center of decent education. No one in the school seemed to mind, since my students stayed in the room and we left everything clean and neat at the end of the day.

However, the pastels got me into trouble. About two months into the semester I got a visit from the district art coordinator, to whom I proudly showed off my students' work. Instead of being encouraged, I was given a copy of the district manual, which described the art curriculum and showed that pastels were a sixth-grade medium. Since my students were in the fifth grade, I was instructed to get rid of both the pastels and the students' work in that medium. I objected and pointed out that the top class in the fifth grade had pastels and used them all the time. The response was that "those" students read above grade level and therefore deserved an advanced art medium, whereas my students read below grade level and therefore weren't qualified for pastels.

I didn't know whether to laugh or argue—it was too absurd. Fortunately the assistant principal, who was more accustomed to the bizarre ways of the school hierarchy, joined us before I could respond. She told the art coordinator that I was a young teacher and that she would take care of everything. Before I left school that day, she called me into her office and gave me advice for surviving within an irrational system. She knew I would not get rid of the pastels, so she suggested I read the curriculum manuals in order to know when I was violating them, and thus to know how to make everything look kosher before a supervisor's visit. She also promised to give me adequate warning so I could continue to do what I felt was best for the children and still look good to the district supervisors. That way, she wouldn't get in trouble. In effect she gave me a way to resist adjusting to unreasonable demands and initiated me into the subversion of the system that most good teachers practice all the time.

That was my first encounter with the choice between conforming to the demands of the system or meeting the needs of my students. It was a lesson in what I have come to call "maladjustment." Sometime in the mid-1960s I encountered the concept of maladjustment in a speech that Martin Luther King, Jr., had given at the University of California, Berkeley, in May 1958. In it he said:

> Modern psychology has a word that is probably used more than any other word. It is the word "maladjusted." Now we all should seek to live a well-adjusted life in order to avoid neurotic and schizophrenic personalities. But there are some things within our social order to which I am proud to be maladjusted and to which I call upon you to be maladjusted. I never intend to adjust myself to segregation and discrimination. I never intend to adjust myself to mob rule. I never intend to adjust myself to the tragic effects of the methods of physical violence and to tragic militarism. I call upon you to be maladjusted to such things.*

In retrospect my experience with pastels, in a small way, represented the same major struggles that Dr. King referred to—issues of privilege and racism. The "good" students at the school were white and upper middle class, and identified as "gifted." They were given privileges and resources that my students, who were mostly poor and predominantly Puerto Rican, were denied—resources such as pastels and reading books that could be used equally well by both groups. I refused to adjust myself to that inequity.

Adjustment is not to be abandoned lightly. It is wonderful to be able to fit comfortably within a family, at work, in culture, or society. Here is the clearest definition of "adjustment" I have been able to find:

> As a beginning definition, we can say that "adjustment" means "the ability of an individual to live harmoniously with his environment—

---

* Martin Luther King, Jr., *I Have a Dream: Writing and Speeches that Changed the World*, ed. James M. Washington (New York and San Francisco: Harper San Francisco / HarperCollins, 1992), p. 33.

physical, social, intellectual, and moral—and with himself, keeping intact his personal integrity." . . . Adjustment is not an end in itself; rather, it is a description of the relation between an individual and . . . (his or her) . . . environment.*

When it is impossible to remain in harmony with one's environment without giving up deeply held moral values, creative maladjustment becomes a sane alternative to giving up altogether. Creative maladjustment consists of breaking social patterns that are morally reprehensible, taking conscious control of one's place in the environment, and readjusting the world one lives in based on personal integrity and honesty—that is, it consists of learning to survive with minimal moral and personal compromise in a thoroughly compromised world and of not being afraid of planned and willed conflict, if necessary. It also means searching for ways of not being alone in a society where the mythology of individualism negates integrity and leads to isolation and self-mutilation. It means small everyday acts of maladjustment as well as occasional major reconstruction, and it requires will, determination, faith that people can be wonderful, conscious planning, and an unshakable sense of humor.

Creative maladjustment is reflective. It implies adapting your own particular maladjustment to the nature of the social systems that you find repressive. It also implies learning how other people are affected by those systems, how personal discontent can be appropriately turned into moral and political action, and how to speak out about the violence that thoughtless adjustment can cause or perpetuate.

Sometimes decisions to maladjust are made without thought and can lead to trouble. Such trouble befell me twice at the beginning of my teaching career. During my six weeks of student teaching I got into trouble for trying things that clashed with the

---

* Fritz Redl and William Wattenberg, *Mental Hygiene in Teaching* (New York: Harcourt, Brace, and World, 1951; 2d ed 1959), p. 185.

style and practice of my supervising teacher. I was accused of getting too close to the students, of being too informal, and of replacing structured learning activities with open-ended, cross-disciplinary projects. When I was asked to do things that in my judgment were detrimental to student learning and self-respect, I changed them without asking permission. This maladjustment made sense in terms of maintaining my integrity and helping students, but it was suicide for a student teacher who didn't have his or her own classroom and who had no status within the school. Two weeks before the end of my student-teaching assignment, I was unceremoniously terminated by the supervising teacher and ordered out of the school by the principal.

It was my luck to have a wonderful, progressive educator as my supervisor at Columbia's Teachers College. She made it clear that I had acted foolishly and reminded me that if I wanted to teach and change the schools I had to get a credential first. Then she placed me in another school for two weeks, enabling me to fulfill my student teaching requirement. This was not formally legal, but she knew how to creatively maladjust within the framework of Teachers College; moreover, she had the power and experience to act within the institution counter to its own rules. Her planned creative maladjustment worked. My unthinking maladjustment failed.

The same thing happened during my first teaching assignment. Pastels were just a part of the problem. I also spoke out about other inequities at the school during faculty and union meetings and was involuntarily transferred to another school at the end of my first semester. At that time my maladjustment was neither creative nor effective, and I continue to wonder how much more useful I might have been to the school and the community had my responses been more tempered and my maladjustment better thought-out.

However, as a beginning teacher I found myself with too much to learn, too little support, and an inflated sense of how much reform I could accomplish by myself without having experience or friends and allies within the community or the school district. I did learn one lesson that semester, though, and it has been at the center of my educational thinking and practice for the last thirty years. As I mentioned, most of my students were Puerto Rican, and almost all of them spoke Spanish as a first language. Back then the official policy of the New York City Board of Education forbade Spanish to be spoken in the classroom. I didn't speak Spanish, though I knew enough French and Italian to make occasional good guesses at what my students were saying. I also didn't have enough confidence or experience to know how to question that policy intelligently.

At that time teachers were obliged to evaluate the linguistic and intellectual skills of all children in English and to determine their ability to read and do arithmetic. It should hardly have been a surprise that the test results indicated that the children's math skills were better than their reading skills. Based on this information a number of researchers drew various conclusions, such as that Spanish-speaking children have better abstract abilities than linguistic ones, that children learn arithmetic independently of their language skills, and so on. However, the researchers neglected (or were ignorant of) one key point in their analysis of the situation: almost all of the children who did well in arithmetic performed equally well at reading Spanish. I discovered this by accident. One day I happened to bring to school a book that had a quotation from García Lorca's *Poeta en Nueva York*, in Spanish, and one of the boys who was unable to read English read the Spanish selection with ease and translated it for me. It was obvious that the attempt to measure his linguistic skills solely through the evaluation of his ability to read and write in English was irrational and cruel.

The same student, Vincente, was a problem in class and a delight before and after school. In class he would fidget and bother other kids. He looked like a tightly wound spring, ready to release and jump through a door, window, or wall. However, when I ran into Vincente on the street or at the small restaurant his parents ran he was charming and showed an incredible awareness of current political and social events. His parents were troubled by his school history. They told me that he had been on the mainland for three years and had done very poorly in school, though he had been a top student in Puerto Rico. They thought maybe it was a matter of language, but they said that the teachers in Puerto Rico cared much more and gave the students much more respect.

I liked Vincente and came to appreciate his intelligence and sensitivity, but he acted nuts in class, performed for the other students, and caused me as much grief as he could. His was the lowermost class in the grade, and all of the students had experienced the humiliation of failure. Their integrity was violated by the institution. Some, like Vincente, decided to get even with the system even though they hurt themselves more than they hurt their teachers or the system.

I was in my early twenties at the time and very inexperienced. I never figured out how to help Vincente, but, through knowing him and several other youngsters in the class outside of school and becoming friends with their parents, I came to understand that children in school act in ways that are shaped by the institution; therefore it is essential never to judge a child by her or his school behavior.

I had to maladjust myself to the notion that the demands and structure of schooling were normal and the students were problems if they did not adjust. This meant examining the nature of the life I was expected to lead as a teacher and sorting out what was sensible and beneficial to my students from procedures meant simply to keep things under control. It meant learning to recognize practices and texts that were racist or sexist, as well as coming to understand the mechanisms for tolerating professional incompetence and for marginalizing children who are outspoken or different. This had to be done while I was figuring out how to teach well, and I had to be creative about it if I wanted to keep my job. I had to develop the skills of creative maladjustment and integrate into every aspect of my teaching the idea that school was not always worth adjusting to and that my students were often right to resist the education being forced upon them.

For me an understanding of the need for creative maladjustment is not a rejection of public education, but an affirmation of its possibilities. It is part of what I subsequently learned has been a long struggle to make public education work for all children. The biggest problems are not with public education itself, but with the attitude that, inasmuch as many public schools don't work, public education should be abandoned, and that because many students are not currently learning, they can't learn. It is our job as educators to make schools work, and that requires taking up the struggle, within the system, to transform them. Dr. King, throughout his life, strived to make democracy work, not to abandon democracy altogether because it wasn't yet working.

Over the years, I have learned how to analyze schools and have tried to figure out their effects on children's behavior rather than judge children by that behavior. This maladjustment has allowed me to reach many children who otherwise would have been remote and hostile. It has also allowed me to shape my teaching by attending to the interaction between the culture of the schools and the larger social, cultural, and economic lives of the children, rather than responding to students' present or past school performance and behavior.

The word "performance" is used in educational circles to indicate test scores and behavior, but for me it is part of an apt and useful theater metaphor. Children are on stage at school, and the teacher is only one of several audiences. Other students, parents, and people in the community are also audiences. Each student faces the simultaneous task of winning the acceptance of each of these audiences while maintaining personal and moral integrity. The construction of a school character is a complex matter with a great deal at stake. Unfortunately schools often simplify the script and divide youngsters into good/bad, normal/abnormal, intelligent/dumb, and high/low potential. This division forces roles on students, ones they only partially play. As a teacher I found it essential to maladjust to dichotomies like these and refuse to allow them to enter into my thoughts or vocabulary. This maladjustment, combined with a *crise de coeur*, inadvertently led me to become involved in the deaf power movement in 1966, four years after I had begun teaching.

I was in graduate school at the time, and it was possible for me to take courses while continuing my work with youngsters in the community where I had previously taught. One of the classes I took, called "Natural Language for the Deaf," advocated a holistic though oralist approach to the education of deaf children. The class was taught by a wonderful woman, whose life was dedicated to the enrichment of learning among deaf youngsters and whose educational philosophy centered around the idea that deaf children will learn to speak best if they are in an informal, conversational situation in which reading, writing, and speaking are integrated.

One day toward the middle of the semester an eight- or nine-year-old girl came to class to demonstrate the effectiveness of this method. Something in my heart responded to her dignity and intensity. When she began to speak to the class about her school, I couldn't understand anything she said. She strained and struggled, but what came out was something resembling, but not quite English. Her face was wracked with tension, and I assumed she was closely listening to her own voice to be sure what she was saying was correct. Suddenly, I realized she couldn't hear herself, couldn't make corrections, and couldn't hear our responses either. Until that moment I had never imagined myself in a world without sound.

Something was wrong here. This girl was obviously intelligent and sensitive—her eyes and gestures made that clear. She was in pain. And she was the best example the school had to show for its attempts at getting deaf youngsters to speak. Something was wrong, not with her but with the educational regime she was living under. It was a situation that begged for maladjustment, that reminded me of frustration I felt at being told not to speak Spanish in my classroom.

I decided to visit the school the young girl attended. Even before entering the school it was impossible not to notice that one was in a sign-language environment. Students getting off the buses or coming out of the subway station were all signing. Young children on the playground were signing. Older ones taking a last puff on their cigarettes or just standing around flirting and gossiping were using sign language. The prohibition on signs began once youngsters were inside; it obviously did not extend into their lives outside of school. Before visiting even one class it was clear that the prohibition of signs in deaf education indicated deep institutional and sociological problems.

This impression was confirmed when I learned that the teachers were all hearing individuals who did not know sign language; that students in this very caring and progressive environment still had to sit on their hands if they inadvertently signed in class; and that the achievement scores of the students at the school were lower than those at schools with a comparable non-deaf middle- and upper-class student body, indicating that some academic connections were not being made. Nevertheless, the staff was very enthusiastic about its work and proud of its success in enabling its students to master spoken English and achieve academically. To me this meant that they had low expectations for their students, accepting barely comprehensible spoken English and below-grade-level scores as excellent work. They had adjusted the school according to coordinates of educational research and philosophy and imposed their grid on the children.

My reading in the literature on the cognitive development of the deaf confirmed my suspicions. Throughout the United States, deaf children were evaluated by researchers who did not sign, were given test instructions in spoken English, and were required to read selections drawn entirely from the nondeaf world. The children were set up for failure and then labeled cognitively deficient. The system stayed in adjustment and the children became ab-normalized.

Fortunately, at that time I stumbled upon a reference to William Stokoe's work on a sign-language dictionary in Louie Fant, Jr.'s book on the National Theater of the Deaf. Not one of the "experts" I consulted was familiar with any serious study of the language of signs other than one written about a hundred years before. Stokoe's early works, which he kindly sent me, were done in the fields of anthropology and sociology and not read by educators. They confirmed my suspicions that the language of signs was indeed a language with a syntax and grammar, and that the entire research apparatus dealing with the education of the deaf was culturally biased and intellectually irresponsible.

I believe there were two underlying reasons for this: first, hearing people controlled the education of the deaf and did not bother to learn sign language; and second, this neglect of sign language was reinforced by the predominantly nondeaf parents of deaf children (there had been a rubella epidemic in the late fifties and early sixties that increased the population of school-age deaf children at the time I was writing the paper). The parents did not want their children to sign and become socially identified as deaf. They wanted their children to adjust to the hearing world. They wanted their children to talk, to be "normal," and educators tried to give them what they wanted even though it was impossible. The consequence was lack of communication and often bitter alienation between nondeaf adults and their deaf children.

The most painful thing I discovered during these explorations was that many parents, by neglecting to learn sign language themselves, gave up the possibility of communicating with their children. Instead, often out of anxiety over their children's' futures, they chose to turn their children over to educators who promised to get their children to speak. Social norming and linguistic adjustment became a barrier between parents and children, something that often happens to immigrant children today.

I wrote a graduate school paper on the language and education of the deaf, concluding that deaf children should be taught in sign language or bilingually, and that the parents of deaf infants would be best served by learning to sign. A year later the paper was published as the booklet *Language and Education of the Deaf*. The response was explosive. The Alexander Graham Bell Association for the Deaf, one of the most powerful forces in the area of deaf education, attacked me as an irresponsible outsider who had no right to intrude into the field of deaf education. At the same time, I was invited to Washington, D.C., to speak about the subject at Gallaudet College, the nation's major institution of higher education for deaf people, and to do a summer program at Kendall Green, the elementary school on the Gallaudet campus.

At dinner before the speech, my wife Judy and I had time to communicate with faculty members from Galluadet. Powrie Doctor, one of the most respected voices in the deaf community and a professor at Gallaudet, spoke to us, a rare event. He was profoundly deaf and had been forced to learn oral language at school. The humiliation of that experience was such that he refused to use it except in special circumstances such as communicating with Judy, myself and other nondeaf friends of the deaf community. He told us at dinner that he could lip-read and speak well enough to join the hearing world but that he had made the conscious decision, as a deaf adult, to maladjust to the hearing world. Martin Luther King, Jr., and other civil right activists were heroes of his, and he had visions of a deaf power movement. What he wanted to do was organize from within the deaf community and build a movement to agitate for a society in which the deaf had control over their own education and made their own decisions about how they would relate to the hearing world. The reason the Bell Association was so outraged about my pamphlet, he informed me, was that once deaf adults understood themselves as victims of a dysfunctional system and became convinced of the intelligence they obviously had, the hearing would no longer be able to control their education and their lives.

Dr. Doctor (that was the way people signed his name) told me that he went through a painful period of personal and social struggle during his withdrawal from the world of the hearing. He had to discover ways of uncovering his strengths while undoing his internalization of the stigma of being "deaf and dumb," and healing the injuries caused by being stared at when he was signing and misunderstood when he spoke. He said he decided not to adjust to being deaf.

Adjusting would have meant fitting into a world managed and controlled by hearing people—a world where he was considered damaged goods. Instead he became part of the adult deaf world where he could live a fuller life while knowing how and choosing when to navigate in the hearing world. He also decided to teach and organize among deaf people and help them learn how to manage the hearing world without being controlled by it.

One of his strategies was to show students how to turn stereotypes of deaf people on their heads—a form of what I've called creative maladjustment. For example, he encouraged his students to take trips on public transportation and observe the gestures and facial expressions of the hearing people around them. Many of these expressions and gestures have meaning in sign language, and Dr. Doctor demonstrated some of the silly, sometimes sexually suggestive or personally embarrassing things hearing people inadvertently sign just by moving their hands or letting an expression pass over their face.

Everyone else at the table cracked up at Dr. Doctor's imitations of hearing people inadvertently signing something silly or embarrassing. I felt excluded from a complex linguistic game. Dr. Doctor, after explaining the jokes, went on to describe the power of such role switching for some of his students. It taught them that they could observe as well as be observed, that stigma was socially constructed, and that they could take a stance toward the hearing world that would not make them feel inferior. Creative maladjustment was one of the tools he used to help his students learn to free themselves from the rage of being under the gaze and control of the hearing world. His goal was to build a community of the deaf that affirmed sign language and was not burdened by the linguistic ignorance and prejudices of the hearing world.

Dr. Doctor was a major inspiration for the deaf power movement, and I'm sure that, over ten years later, when students at Gallaudet walked out of classes, demanded, and won the battle for a deaf president of the college, he must have been laughing in whatever heaven there is for the creatively maladjusted.

The publisher of *Language and Education of the Deaf* received dozens of letters responding in particular to my advocacy of sign language in schools. Some questioned my credentials to write about deaf education. Others called for a deaf power movement. A few were from hearing parents who thanked me for giving them the courage to learn sign language. It opened up a world of communication with their deaf children, they wrote, whereas before there had been only silence and grief.

I like to think I had some small part in the deaf power movement, which has succeeded in changing many of the stereotypes about the intellectual and linguistic capacities of deaf people, and has permanently rid the "dumb" from "deaf and dumb." I have not had much to do with the education of the deaf since 1968, but the idea has stayed with me that the way students behave is as much a consequence of the system in which they are required to learn as anything within themselves, their families, communities, and cultures. The task of helping my students figure out how to creatively maladjust to dysfunctional systems of living and learning has become a significant part of my work as an educator.

In fact, I can imagine classes in creative maladjustment at teacher education institutions, for without teachers who are willing to take the risks on creative maladjustment, public education will continue to fail or be dismantled and privatized.

Recently I found myself trying to provoke my students into adopting precisely that stance toward their future work. I was teaching an undergraduate class, entitled "Introduction to Education," at Hamline University in St. Paul, Minnesota. This was the first class in the sequence for prospective teachers, and my students were prospective elementary or secondary school teachers. The first writing assignment I gave the class was to describe a very good or very bad learning experience they had had. Half of the papers described good experiences, the others horrible ones.

The "good" learning experiences involved some teacher who had gone out of her or his way to support, challenge, befriend, or encourage the student as an individual. These teachers broke through the impersonality that was the daily round of my students' lives in school and paid attention to their inner needs, aspirations, and problems. The "bad" experiences all dealt with humiliation, with teachers picking out and putting down students for getting things wrong or not understanding what was being taught.

In class discussion it came out that almost all of the students in my class were thinking about becoming public school teachers either to give their students the gifts they had received from a kind teacher who had inspired them, or to protect them from what the sociologist Edgar Freidenberg calls the "ritual humiliations of schooling" and the consequent feelings of stupidity and shame.

As a result of my students' responses I decided to spend the first two weeks of class speculating about personalized education and strategies for the elimination of humiliation in the classroom. I wanted to help the students articulate their own philosophies of education before introducing them to other ideas that might broaden their concept of what education might be. However, most of the students found these discussions boring and wanted me to tell them what textbook to read, what the schedule of assignments was, and how my grading system compared with that of the professor who usually taught the class. Above all, they wanted predictability, regularity, and class rankings. They had been well schooled though not necessarily well educated.

Almost all of the members of the class resisted my attempts to set an analytic and personalized context for their future teaching. A number of them had already obtained last year's texts, tests, and answers from friends. They had "scoped" out the course beforehand and found that, with a little work, they could score an A. This was a relief in their busy academic schedules. However, they didn't know that they would have a professor with different goals and outcomes in mind, and they resented it.

The students wanted to know what the right answers were, and I wanted to talk about the questions. There was a period of two weeks where the class was a dismal place. The resistance to what I was doing was palpable, and I spent hours worrying about how to reach the students without giving in to their desire for status quo education. Despite the stories they told in their papers, they had not thought much about the web that ties humiliation, grading, and closed questioning into a system of depersonalized education. I was convinced that giving in to their desires for textbooks, tests, and lectures would not help them become the teachers they dreamed of being.

It was time to introduce creative maladjustment into the classroom, and I found a way to do it at the checkout stand of Rainbow Supermarket in St. Paul. I have always been intrigued by gossip and scandal newspapers, especially those that trade in absurd claims. There is a perverse intelligence at work in the creation of headlines such as "Survivors of Titanic Found Picnicking on Iceberg," "Hitler Runs Delicatessen in Buenos Aires," and

"Mink Coat Eats Owner." One night, while I was worrying about the lack of progress in my class, I saw the following headline: "Baby Boy Born With a Wooden Leg." I read the accompanying article and decided to integrate it into my curriculum. I bought the paper and shared the article with my class. Their assignment for the week was to get a copy of the paper, read the article, and write a three-page paper that would substantiate or deny its claims.

The students, to my thorough astonishment, took me perfectly seriously and behaved as if I had given them another essay by Piaget to analyze. It was a tribute to the effectiveness of the current educational system that any nonsense handed out by an authority figure would be taken seriously. The students' responses were equally surprising. Some contained serious arguments about whether a baby could actually be born with a peg leg. Others were discussions of reincarnation. A few tried to make logical arguments about why the article couldn't possibly be true, while two claimed that it had to be true because scientists and a doctor were cited.

No one came right out and said that they thought I was putting them on with the assignment. The class discussion was quite different than usual. I noticed puzzlement and the kind of emotional stress that often leads to productive thinking. What is this crazy man asking us to do?

I was breaking the pattern, provoking questions, having them read an article from a paper they at first claimed they had never read but later on admitted they looked at in the supermarket. They were scared by the point I was making about authority and intelligence, and by the mode of question-posing and creative maladjustment that I was introducing as an alternative to right answers.

I realized that in this context it would be very easy to humiliate the class, to show them up as being silly, which was the opposite of my intent. Instead of dealing directly with their responses I decided to raise the issue of the doctor and the scientists referred to in the article. Who were they? How did one judge their authority or know if they even existed? Can print lie? When and why?

Over the next few days we had discussions about how to evaluate the claims made by experts, books, journals, and the media. The theme evolved into a consideration of how to develop trust in one's own mind, judgment, and experience. And then I turned to the tension between unquestioned acceptance of authority and creative maladjustment, and to its educational implications.

The ability to break patterns and pose new questions is as important as the ability to answer questions other people set for you. This is as true for teachers who care about their students as it is for the students themselves. It requires the courage to create a bold disruption of routines of thought and practice and implies a healthy love of turning the world upside down—which is very difficult in an academic situation driven by grades.

A central teaching skill consists of detecting and analyzing dysfunctional patterns of obedience and learning, and developing strategies to negate them. It means that teachers have to become sophisticated pattern detectives and sleuth out ways in which the practices they have been taught—or have inherited—inhibit learning.

Unfortunately, the momentum of educational research and the attempt to turn education into a single, predictable, and controllable system with national standards and national tests pulls in the opposite direction. Teaching well is a militant activity that requires a belief in children's strengths and intelligence no matter how poorly they may function under the regimens imposed upon them. It requires understanding student failure as system failure, especially when it encompasses the majority of students in a class, school, or school system. It also means stepping back and seeing oneself as a part of a dysfunctional system and developing the courage to maladjust rather than adjust oneself to much of current educational practice. This means seeing oneself as a worker in a large system run amok and giving up the need to defend the system to yourself or in public. And, in the service of one's students, it might even involve risking one's job and career. There are limits to creative maladjustment within the system, and they sometimes drive one to act, in the service of public education, from outside the system. But it is possible to defend public education without having to defend the public schools as they currently exist.

Recently I taught a graduate school teacher education class called "Using Words Well." The class, for practicing teachers, was predicated on the idea that young people need the opportunity to speak about ideas and experience with each other rather than constantly be asked to respond to set questions. Toward the end of the class we had an intense discussion about ways in which time can be found in the classroom for students to learn how to speak well and intelligently. Most of the teachers said there was no way they could fit in open-ended conversation because they were being held to student time on task and learning outcomes—that is, to working at measurable tasks using controlled materials without a moment for thought, reflection, or discussion. The net in which teachers and students had been caught was of a very fine mesh. There were no spaces available for the free flow of ideas and stories. The pattern of life in their classrooms inhibited the development of their students and quieted their own enthusiasm for teaching. The last part of the class was devoted to ways of breaking out of the net, ways of sneaking in love of language and the joy of communication.

"Baby Boy Born With a Wooden Leg"—the use of absurdity with a straight face—was foreign to these teachers' styles and classroom personalities. We had to figure out other ways to help them break the patterns. Teachers are rarely encouraged in an educational setting to speculate on what is absurd in their own work. That would be unprofessional. But we were nonprofessional with joy.

The teachers in the class came up with their own strategies for pattern-breaking in the classroom. One teacher said that she would not grade the most important paper of the year but ask for revisions instead. Another decided that the reward for finishing assignments would not be time off but time on—that is, she would allow students to get into issue discussion groups and mural projects. A third decided that half of all formal class assignments could be fulfilled by writing ungraded novels and poetry instead. And all came up with a commitment to talk for at least fifteen minutes a day about something happening in the world or something of a sensitive nature that was on the students' minds.

One member of the class said that all of these proposals were steps into sanity. His district had been bombarded with outcome-based learning, alternative and standard assessments, national standards in all subjects, and other such nonsense. He was ready to fight back but needed a first step into maladjustment—that is, working specifically and consciously on breaking sanctioned though dysfunctional patterns of learning. He said he was going to come to school early one day, pile up all of the chairs and desks and push them in the corner. Then, when the students came, he would begin class as if nothing unusual had happened and leave it to the students to respond. He did it a few weeks later and told me that he was probably the most nervous person in the room but that once one of the students asked what was going on, there was an animated discussion of his actions and a permanent reorganization of the room.

This is not a small thing. It is a powerful first lesson in breaking the pattern for both students and teacher. It provides a sense that it is possible to go beyond what authorities tell you to do and that you can cross boundaries and create new forms of association. However, it is a private act performed behind closed classroom doors. The next steps in creative maladjustment are more difficult. They involve reaching out to other teachers and to the community the school serves, engaging others in the struggle to create decent and effective schools, becoming a leader in your own school and community, and taking responsibility for that role.

There are a number of specific things people within and outside of public education can do in defense of public education. One essential step is to seek out and find good practice-schools or classrooms that work within the public schools. As educators we must articulate and defend what we consider to be good practice. This is difficult when you are part of a system that has produced so much failure. Nevertheless there are good examples of public education that works and books that document them, such as *Embracing Diversity*, edited by Laurie Olsen (San Francisco: California Tomorrow, 1991); *The Good Common School: Making the Vision Work for All Children* (Boston, MA: National Coalition of Advocates for Students, 1992); and George Wood, *Schools that Work: America's Most Innovative Public Education Programs* (New York: Dutton, 1992). The journal *Rethinking Schools* (1001 E. Keefe Ave., Milwaukee, WI, 53212) is also a marvelous source of information about current school struggles and the excellent work one can find within public education.

Create a library of good practice for yourself and your school. One form of creative maladjustment is to be literate and knowledgeable about what is going on in public education throughout the country and to share that knowledge with teachers' organizations and the community.

In addition, it is our responsibility as educators to examine all of the categories of educational stigma and to stand against anything that damages our students or limits their life possibilities—for example, programs whose funding depends on a perpetual supply of failing students. In the early 1970s I was asked to help a group of Chicano college students in southern California set up a reading and writing program in a local public school. The school district had agreed to enter into a partnership with the college, and several third- and fourth-grade classes were chosen for the experiment. Almost all of the children in the classes were "Title IV" children—that is, they were poor, predominantly minority students who were functioning below grade level and therefore qualified for extra federal funding under Title IV of the Elementary and Secondary Education Act of 1964. The federal money was to be used to support the program.

After a year of hard work the program began to bear fruit. One by one, and then in small groups, the students began to perform on grade level until a critical mass of about two-thirds of the students involved were on or above grade level. At that point some of the college students called and asked me to return to southern California to help plan the next step, which was to expand their program up to the fifth and sixth, and down to the first and second grades.

A few days before my visit I received another call telling me that the program had been cancelled. I asked what had happened and was told that since the program succeeded in getting a number of third and fourth graders up to grade level, those students no longer qualified for Title IV money. The district's Title IV budget was cut, and there was no more financial support for the program. It had to close down. The school-district administration was angry at the students and the college for messing up its supplemental funding. One of the district administrators even remarked at a public meeting that the district had to get the number of its Title IV–qualified students back up in order to maintain its programs. In less than one full academic year the school had reconstituted enough failure to get its full Title IV funding again.

Title IV programs, and other programs that tie money to student failure, do not have a mechanism to deal with success. Programs such as this should be tied to equity issues and centered around the maintenance of quality education rather than the temporary remediation of deficiencies. A creative, though maladjusted, response to such programs should be the writing of enabling legislation and the political mobilization of teachers and communities in support of continued good education rather than remedial programs.

The strategy of stigmatizing children as a cover for educational incompetency is not, however, limited to children of the poor. The primary victims of this syndrome are middle-class children who can perform academically but refuse to do so when they are not challenged. The category was invented as an extension of the idea that as educators we do not need to examine our practice and change it when it fails. Recently a new category of stigma has been constructed: Attention Deficit Disorder. Students designated as ADD often refuse to sit still and listen silently when a teacher or another person in authority is talking; they resist following instructions blindly; they refuse to do boring worksheets and other assignments if they feel they already know the material. Interestingly enough, these conditions are positive qualifications for future participatory citizenship, and an argument can be made that ADD is one way that public school authorities are suppressing the spirit of democracy.

In his well-documented book on the educationally handicapped (EH), *The Learning Mystique*, the neurologist Gerald Coles establishes that there is no physiological or medical condition common to all EH children. His remarks hold true for ADD as well. According to Coles, EH is not a condition of brain pathology.

Once designated EH, children are removed from their usual classrooms for the whole or part of the day; some of them are drugged with ritalin; most of them are subjected to simplified versions of the learning material that they had already failed to master in their original classrooms. The special classes they are sometimes sent to are smaller than regular classes, and funded through special laws and regulations providing for special education. The teachers are EH specialists, which means that they took special classes in college on the education of "the EH child" and have certificates, or even master's degrees, in the field—and those college classes are usually taught by professors who have themselves specialized in EH education. However, the substance of what is taught in classes on the education of the EH child is not much different than what is taught in ordinary teacher-education classes.

Thus the EH child is surrounded by an entire social system entailing laws, regulations, funding, college classes, degrees, and certification. The inability of regular classrooms to educate all children (and in particular minority and working-class and poor children) has led to the creation of a profession that depends on children being pushed out of "normal" classrooms and made pathological. Programs that depend on the stigmatization of children (including those at universities that certify teachers to certify children as deficient) must be opposed by creatively maladjusted educators. Teacher education institutions are very sensitive to what they refer to as "pressure from the profession," and speaking out at professional meetings and writings letters of complaint to schools of education about the institutionalization of stigmatization can be very effective. So can the refusal of a classroom teacher to refer any student to special education.

The existence of the EH social subsystem in the schools has not led to a wide-scale increase in the levels of performance of children designated EH. In fact, once the idea is established that school failure is always the fault of the child and that one can get away with blaming the victims of failed practice, the way is open for the constant creation of new categories of pathological behavior as well as for a proliferation of new professions. When school failure reaches massive proportions, the climate is created for going beyond the creation of individual systems of pathology. Categories of social stigmatization are then developed, which turns societal prejudices into pseudoscientific systems of behavior control. We are now at that point. The category of "at risk," though applied to individual children, is a form of social stigmatization that is often difficult to distinguish from racism and class bias.

It is hard to find a clear definition of "at risk" or of "at risk behavior." The clearest definition I've seen appears in the book *At-Risk, Low-Achieving Students in the Classroom*, by Judy Brown Lehr and Hazel Wiggins Harris. The authors admit at the very beginning of Chapter One that "a review of the literature does not indicate a published definition of the at-risk, low-achieving student." Then they go on to give a list of possible labels for the "at-risk, low-achieving student." Here are some of the labels they come up with:

> disadvantaged, culturally deprived, underachiever, non achiever, low ability, slow learner, less able, low socioeconomic status, language-impaired, dropout-prone, alienated, marginal, disenfranchised, impoverished, underprivileged, low-performing and remedial.*

The authors then go on to list characteristics that can be used to identify students at risk (all of which need not be present, they tell us, in order to identify an at-risk student):

> ... academic difficulties, lack of structure (disorganized), inattentiveness, distractibility, short attention span, low self-esteem, health problems, excessive absenteeism, dependence, discipline problem, narrow

---

*Judy Brown Lehr and Hazel Wiggins Harris, *At-Risk, Low-Achieving Students in the Classroom* (Washington, D.C.: National Education Association, 1990), p. 9.

range of interest, lack of social skills, inability to face pressure, fear of failure (feels threatened by learning), and lack of motivation.*

The whole question of identifying at-risk students is itself risky business. To identify children as "at risk" is to pick them out for special treatment *not for what they have done but for what they might do*. A child who is merely doing poorly in school is not necessarily at risk. Nor is a child who has a strong will and a sense of cultural pride and self-respect that she or he feels is violated by the circumstances of schooling.

What makes a child at risk? What is the hidden agenda of the people who have manufactured the "at-risk" category? What are at-risk children at risk of doing? In plain language, at-risk children are at risk of turning the poverty and prejudice they experience against society rather than learning how to conform and take their "proper" place. The children are maladjusting, and it is their teachers' role to make that maladjustment functional and creative rather than to suppress it.

One powerful way for educators to creatively maladjust is to repudiate all categories and assume responsibility for changing their practice until it works for the children they have previously been unable to serve. Another is to advocate genuine educational choice within the public schools and to demand that teachers, parents, and other groups of educators should have the right to create small schools within the context of large public school systems, with the freedom and resources to operate effectively.

There are risks in becoming creatively maladjusted. You might get fired or find projects you have nurtured into existence destroyed by a threatened bureacracy or conservative school board. You might find yourself under pressure at school and at home to stop making trouble and feel like giving in to the temptation to re-adjust and become silent. The choice of when, where,

---

* Ibid., p. 11.

how, and whether to maladjust is both moral and strategic, and though it has social and educational consequences, it is fundamentally personal and private.

For those of us who choose to remake the schools and reaffirm the need for equity, decency, creativity, and openness within public education, walking the line between survival and moral action is a constant and often unnerving challenge. We have to think about being part of an opposition within the system and be articulate and explicit in that role. We have to reach out and develop allies and not be afraid to encounter and confront school boards, administrators, and our own unions with clear positions on educational issues backed by first-rate practice. And we must remember and affirm what we often tell our students: that we can become the people we would like to be, that it is necessary to live with hope, and that it is possible to create a decent life and a decent world.